Blessed is the one who reads . . .

Revelation 1:3

*We are said to drink the blood of Christ
not only in the rite of the sacraments, but also
when we receive his words, in which are life.*

Origen of Alexandria,
Homily on Numbers 16.9.2 (third century)

*Scripture is, if I may put it this way,
a kind of river that is both shallow and deep,
in which a lamb may wade
and an elephant may swim.*

St. Gregory the Great, *Morals on Job*,
Preface to Leander of Seville, iv (sixth century)

Unfolding Sacred Scripture

How Catholics Read the Bible

MICHAEL CAMERON

LITURGY TRAINING PUBLICATIONS

Nihil Obstat
Very Reverend Daniel A. Smilanic, JCD
Vicar for Canonical Services
Archdiocese of Chicago
August 5, 2015

Imprimatur
Very Reverend Ronald A. Hicks
Vicar General
Archdiocese of Chicago
August 5, 2015

This book was edited by Lorie Simmons. Christian Rocha was the production editor, Anna Manhart was the designer, and Luis Leal was the production artist.

Ambo from Bitonto Cathedral in Italy, 1229. Photo © Adrian Fletcher, www.paradoxplace.com. Used with Permission. *Pilgrims of Emmaus on the Road*, opaque watercolor over graphite by James Tissot, 1836–1902. Courtesy of Brooklyn Museum. *Virgin reading*, tempera paint on canvas by Vittore Carpaccio, 1505–1510. National Gallery, Washington DC. Photo from Wikimedia Commons, public domain. *St. Thomas Aquinas reading*, panel painting by Gentile da Fabriano, 1370–1427, from the Valle Romita Polyptych in the Pinacoteca di Brera in Milan. Wikimedia Commons, public domain (The Yorck Project). *St. Augustine as bishop, reading*, tempera on panel, by Antonello da Messina, 1430-7, Galleria Regionale della Sicilia, Palermo. Wikimedia Commons, public domain (The Yorck Project). *Christ Giving His Blessing*, Hans Memling, 1478, oil on oak panel. Painting is in the public domain. Located in the Norton Simon Museum, Pasadena, California. Wikimedia Commons. *Bamberg Apocalypse*, folio 3r. Reproduction in the public domain. Manuscript located in the Bamberg Staatsbibliothek, (MS A. II. 42). Wikimedia Commons.

22 21 20 19 18   2 3 4 5 6

Printed in the United States of America

Library of Congress Control Number: 2015947968

ISBN 978-1-61671-244-0

LBUSS

I dedicate this book to two groups:

First to my dear friends from the early years
of the Chicago Catholic Scripture School of the
Archdiocese of Chicago (1999–2002). They
brought gifts of adventurous trust and a lively
love for Scripture that I will always treasure.

Then to my students at the University of Portland
in sections of my introductory course
"Biblical Tradition and Culture" (2002–2012) and
"The Bible: Past and Present" (2012–2015).
Their fresh-faced inquisitiveness has made the
course new every semester.

I also wish to thank L. N. S. for her encouragement
and care through the time of writing.

CONTENTS

ABBREVIATIONS

DV   *Dogmatic Constitution on Divine Revelation (Dei Verbum)*

IBC   Interpretation of the Bible in the Church

SC   *Constitution on the Sacred Liturgy (Sacrosanctum Concilium)*

PART I

The Catholic Way
of Reading Scripture

CHAPTER 1

Reading the Bible in Catholic Perspective

Yearning for the Word

A magnificent heritage glistens all around us. We see it in our spectacular display of beautiful churches, art, and music, the splendor of our liturgy, our hallowed traditions of learning, service, and spirituality, our galaxy of saints and holy women and men, lay and religious, who have shaped history and changed the world. As Catholics we constantly wear that heritage like an invisible crown. Chances are, however, that we aren't thinking much about that spiritual crown when we're just trying to make it out the door to Mass on Sunday. Yet it's always there, waiting for us to see it and savor it.

One of the great jewels of that crown often escapes the notice of even attentive Catholics: the Bible. We regularly hear biblical readings in church, but may not realize that the entire Mass is saturated in Scripture. Those who do soon feel the urge to read Scripture for themselves. The spoon feedings of each Sunday's readings make us want to go back to the full texts for more. But that family Bible is so big and forbidding, and who has time to read these days? And where to start? Who can stand all those genealogies and laws?

Whatever the reasons, for most Catholics the Bible is a mystery to be opened up—someday. But for you, since you've picked up this book, perhaps "someday" is today. This book unfolds in two parts. Part I is a description of a distinctive Catholic approach to reading Scripture. Part II offers a reading guide for working into the best entry-level parts of the Bible, the narratives.

That being the case, this book will not include chapters on two major non-narrative sections of the Bible: the poetry-based prophetic books of the Old Testament and the letters of the New Testament. To get at the basic story line about Jesus, the book will treat only the first three "synoptic" Gospel narratives of Matthew, Mark, and Luke, and not the advanced symbolic narrative of the Gospel according to John. The chapters on apocalyptic texts of the Bible are included for the way they advance and round off the narratives of the two Testaments.

Learning the stories of the Bible is the basic building block for learning to read well, and a platform for further investigation. If you work with this book and a good study Bible, you will gain what you need to get started. You will grasp Scripture's central story line, its main characters, dramatic twists, and important concepts, and gain enough know-how to begin reading and understanding the Bible for yourself—*as a Catholic*. Welcome to the journey.

You have many fellow travelers. Catholics are hungrier than ever to read the Bible. Before the Second Vatican Council (1962–1965), many Catholics felt discouraged from reading the Bible without official help, but the Church now strongly encourages people to pursue what medieval thinkers called "the sacred page" (*sacra pagina*). Encouragement for scholarly study of the Bible had begun to trickle out from Pope Leo XIII in the late nineteenth century, became a stream with Pope Pius XII in the mid-twentieth, and then became a flowing river at the Second Vatican Council. Council documents like *The Dogmatic Constitution on Divine Revelation* (*Dei Verbum*) (1965)[1] offer a wonderfully rich and very readable starting place for gaining a Catholic sense of Scripture. The Council Fathers wanted to make Scripture accessible to everyone, and commended the best and most up-to-date historical, literary, and theological scholarship.

The Council Fathers wanted to make Scripture accessible to everyone.

---

1. In references, abbreviated as DV.

Catholics soon emerged in the top tier of academic biblical scholarship, which before that had been populated only by Protestants. Superior works of Catholic biblical scholarship appeared, like *The Jerome Biblical Commentary* (1968; updated as *The New Jerome Biblical Commentary*, 1990). Preaching became much more biblically focused. *The Lectionary for Mass*, which determines the schedule of Scripture readings, was revised after the Council (published in the United States in 1972) to provide more readings of Scripture on a rotating three-year basis. Ever more abundant streams of Catholic biblical works for scholars, clergy, and interested laypeople began to flow from Catholic publishing houses. Some dioceses began to sponsor systematic Bible study programs like the four-year programs of the Denver Catholic Biblical School, the Hartford Catholic Biblical School, and the Chicago Catholic Scripture School. Parishes wanting to foster Scripture groups can now choose from a variety of Catholic Bible study resources, and many people have had transformative experiences in these settings. And yet, and yet . . .

Studies show that the promise and excitement of the Catholic Scripture renewal has not funneled down to average Mass-goers as fully as hoped. By far most Catholics still encounter Scripture only at church, even if they own a Bible at home. An interesting recent study commissioned by the American Bible Society and the Barna Group, entitled "The State of the Bible 2013: A Study of U.S. Adults," found that ninety-eight percent of "practicing Catholics" (defined minimally as attending Mass at least once a month) own a Bible; however, the number of those who read it more than once a week (not including readings at Mass) drops to twenty-nine percent. (Of these "active" Catholics, forty-five percent read less than five times a year, and twelve percent not at all.) The number of practicing Catholics surveyed who consider themselves "highly knowledgeable" is only eight percent (thirty-two percent call themselves "moderately knowledgeable").

Many parishes offer no opportunities for group study of Scripture. Even when they do, the percentage of people participating is relatively tiny. Some years ago one survey put the number of

Catholics participating in group-related Scripture study at less than ten percent. The American Bible Society-Barna study reported a figure of thirty-three percent. The higher number seems to suggest an upswing, but in any case the numbers are low. Why is that?

Perhaps Catholics feel they get "enough Bible" at church. And yet it must be said that the readings at Mass are only small snippets cut from much larger texts, and they are rarely self-explanatory. They reflect ancient history, perhaps strange cultural practices, some unfamiliar words and phrasing, different forms of literature (history, poetry, letters, and so forth). Moreover, even when proclaimed well, the readings go by all too quickly. Stories may come through well enough, but their background and connections to the other readings are not always obvious, and who can take in one of those complicated readings from St. Paul in a single hearing? Without learning these texts outside Mass, many of the nuances and echoes of these readings—some of astonishing depth and beauty—simply go by the boards or over our heads.

This puts some bite into St. Jerome's famous comment, "Ignorance of Scripture is ignorance of Christ." He was referring less to doctrinal definitions of Christ for the mind and more to the personal sense of Christ for faith and life. The spiritual blank drawn by many Catholics from the Scripture readings at Mass represents not just a missed opportunity for knowledge, but also a loss of vital nutrients for faith, as well as a tragic blockage of wisdom and deep comfort in times of stress. We perish for thirst while floating on a lake of refreshment. The liturgical seasons and especially good homilies help to supply some of what's missing; but Mass isn't a Bible study, and anyway, it's impossible to give adequate explanations for the four different Scripture readings at a Mass (including the psalm). Catholics with a serious desire to know Scripture have to go beyond Sunday Mass.

Ignorance of Scripture is ignorance of Christ.

—St. Jerome

How does that happen? More popular and accessible options are available than ever before, and they are multiplying; the obvious example is what's become available on the Internet, as close as a click. On the other hand, in the cyber jungle, anyone can set up a webpage and claim to be an authority on Scripture. Who knows what's good and what isn't? But pent-up hunger naturally seeks nourishment wherever it can be found, so not uncommonly Catholics turn to quite un-Catholic and in some cases anti-Catholic resources on the Internet and elsewhere.

The American Bible Society-Barna study revealed other interesting observations about Catholic Bible readers. Among surveyed "practicing" Roman Catholics who read the Bible on a regular basis, by far the largest percentage (twenty-seven percent) read not a recommended Catholic translation, but some form of the King James Version. This is the classic Shakespearean-era English translation (1611) that remains the most popular version of the Bible among all Christian readers, but especially Protestant evangelicals (this includes the *New KJV* with updated English). By contrast, only nine percent of regular Catholic readers use the official Catholic translation, the *New American Bible,* and other approved Catholic translations like *The New Jerusalem Bible* didn't make the list at all (less than one percent). That seems to indicate that many Roman Catholics looking for serious Bible knowledge often look to evangelical Protestants, who often claim authority to explain the Bible and offer easily available, user-friendly resources in print, online, and in other media.

Is this a problem? No one should disparage any sources of basic Bible knowledge, or scoff at restless spirits trying to learn how to read Scripture, however it happens. Catholics can find very good basic help like maps and book outlines and word studies that are perfectly compatible with being Catholic; and the model of dedicated discipline to reading Scripture daily offers much to be admired and imitated. But it's hard to go it alone like that. Catholics using these sites for getting grounded in Scripture also risk getting a subtle message that derides them for knowing so little and reminds them how little their Catholic community seems to value what they're doing.

What makes the evangelical approach attractive, and why is it so successful among Catholics? Perhaps the evangelical sense of certainty about the Bible mirrors the Catholic sense of certainty about the Church, and that likeness makes crossovers quite easy.[2] But also, certain aspects of the evangelical Bible experience are naturally and spontaneously appealing. Faithful evangelicals feel that the Bible speaks to them with endearing *intimacy*, with the immediacy of a close friend. Further, evangelical readers believe in the Bible's self-evident *clarity*. The Bible's authority is neatly plain and direct, this perspective suggests; you need not go through a priest or church or some other authority to get permission for what to think, particularly about something so vital to one's eternal destiny. This leads to the "blessed assurance" (to use the title of Fanny Crosby's famous camp meeting song) of evangelical *certainty*. A favorite saying is, "God said it; I believe it; that settles it." The Bible speaks with the voice of an unchallengeable *authority*, and memorizing many tried-and-true quotes provides a sense of reliable coverage on many issues. The promise of immediate insight inspires confidence that allows the Bible to be the perfect guide to life's questions and ambiguities. See the neat list of biblical solutions to personal problems in the first pages of your hotel room's Gideon's Bible, in a section called "Bible Helps." The obvious immediacy and potency that many texts really do have go straight to one's heart, and spark devotion, assurance, comfort, and peace, and that continually reinforces the truth of this way of reading. In this view, the institutional Church's abstract and impersonal concern to back up its own teachings undervalues the earnest seeker's independent Holy Spirit-driven sense of what is true

---

2. For the sake of full disclosure: I was raised Catholic, but became part of the Protestant world in my young adulthood. For a while I was part of an evangelical church, but later moved to the more mainstream Presbyterian Church U.S.A., which ordained me to pastoral ministry. In time I rediscovered my roots and returned to the Roman Catholic Church, but have always felt that the best of my Protestant experience came back with me. Many evangelicals are among my friends and family.

for *this* moment in *my* life. Moreover, unlike churches, priests, friends, or even one's own family, the Bible is *always accessible*. Ever handy in your purse or pocket, it gives instantaneous counsel and comfort with the constancy of an all-night food mart. It's easy to see why this approach to Bible reading *does work* on the personal level, and much good can be gained from it—as far as it goes.

How Is a Catholic Reading of Scripture Different?

First, let it be said you are not required to reject anything good coming from your investment in Bible reading, wherever you got it. However, the Catholic tradition offers an "added value," something different and unique: its characteristic "both-and" approach seamlessly and skillfully

The Catholic approach holds together Scripture's divine and human aspects and its readers' intellectual, emotional, and moral needs.

holds together Scripture's divine and human aspects, its spiritual and fleshly dimensions, and its readers' intellectual, emotional, and moral needs. Where evangelical approaches double down on the personal and remain wary of external, historical, and institutional commitments, Catholic thinking and experience holds these together: the authenticity and warmth of personally discovered truth *and* the stability, security, and depth of a historic communal tradition. Moreover, it insists that *this very work of holding the two together is deeply biblical.* So learning to read Scripture as a Catholic does not require denigrating other points of view, nor does it insist that its way is right just because it's Catholic. The Catholic way of reading Scripture, at least at its best, is characterized by the strength, fullness, breadth, and width of its embrace of all God's revelation and the whole human person. I will call this way of reading "sacramental."

CHAPTER 2

Ten Characteristics
of the Catholic Sacramental Way
# of Reading Scripture

Here are ten characteristics of the Catholic sacramental way of reading Scripture, with some supporting quotes from writers in the Catholic tradition. Mention on this list does not mean that a certain characteristic is unique to Roman Catholicism; other traditions may share in some of these characteristics as well. Catholicism at its best would include all these items in its sacramental way of reading Scripture. The list is hardly comprehensive; it introduces some of the most distinctive themes of a Catholic reading of Scripture.

1. We Find in Scripture That Christ Meets Us Everywhere

We can see the first elements of a Christian reading of Scripture in the Easter day scenes of Luke 24 where the Risen Jesus teaches Scripture to his disciples. It seems to have been the Lord's major activity all day. First he met incognito with the disciples on the road to Emmaus and "interpreted to them things about himself in all the scriptures" (Luke 24:27). They marveled at how Jesus "opened" the Scriptures to them and made their hearts burn (24:32). Then appearing to Peter and all the Apostles, Jesus "opened their minds" (24:45) to understand how he had fulfilled "everything written about [him] in the law of Moses, and in the prophets, and in the psalms" (24:44). The disciples learned to read Israel's Scriptures anew from a completely different vantage point, by reading them, as it were, through the eyes of Jesus, crucified and risen.

This different, "spiritual" text of Scripture with Christ at the center is the one that Christians read, pray, and savor to this day—and not the Jewish Scriptures as such (though they are its basis). We can see this in the way virtually every page of the New Testament puts Christ at the center of the Scriptures of Israel. The "Old Testament" is not read on its own terms, in terms of Israel's ancient history and teachings alone, but as a kind of treasury of teachings for something completely new, the redemption offered by Jesus Christ. See, for example, Peter's references to the prophets and the psalms as pointing to Christ in his sermon on the day of Pentecost (Acts 2:14–36). Or take Paul's even more elaborate interpretations of Israel and the Exodus in 1 Corinthians 10:1–11, when Israel drank water "from a spiritual rock that followed them, and the rock was Christ" (verse 4). Paul concludes (verse 11) by saying that everything that happened to Israel was "written down *as a warning to us* [emphasis added; literally, "typically for us," that is, as a pattern for our instruction], upon whom the end of the ages has come."

This approach raises some theological difficulties, some unresolved since the days of the Apostles. Since what we call the Old Testament came from the Jews, we must grant integrity to the quite different way they read the texts. We should also learn to switch gears and appreciate the meanings of those texts for their original readers in addition to reading them through the Christian lens. And we should be candid that our "Old Testament" was made a *Christian* book from their texts, and in that sense actually serves as the first book of the New Testament.

As Pope Benedict XVI pointed out in his rich and very readable 2010 apostolic exhortation, *The Word of the Lord* (*Verbum Domini*), for us God's Word is not first the Bible; it is rather Jesus Christ, the eternal Word, who took flesh for us and for our salvation. When we acclaim the readings at Mass with, "the word of the Lord," it is by derivation, because they communicate him who is the primary Word of God. Indeed the Church teaches, "Christ speaks whenever the Scriptures are read in the Church."[1] This is its *divine* dimension.

Our Lord is central not only to Scripture's content but also to its very structure. His coming into our world as Word of God in flesh exactly parallels Scripture's own divine-human quality. God, almighty and divine, uses human means to reveal himself to humanity: "For the words of God, expressed in human language, have been made like human discourse, just as the word of the eternal Father, when He took to Himself the flesh of human weakness, was in every way made like men."[2] In Scripture, the divine and human dimensions coexist and are ever present, and they always relate to Christ. For this reason, the Catholic way of reading does not make the text of the Bible an end in itself, but rather looks *through* the text to find the true and full revelation of the Word of God, our Lord Jesus Christ.

This approach to reading Scripture was articulated by early Christian theologians. St. Irenaeus, a second-century bishop of Lyons, first laid out the basic building blocks of the Catholic way of reading Scripture. That is, he unfolded the full meaning of the perspective of Jesus as we see it enacted in Luke 24 when Jesus taught Scripture to the disciples. Irenaeus' most famous book, *Against Heresies*, among other things, is a spirited attack on an unorthodox way of reading Scripture that claimed to have private access to Christ's truth. Irenaeus responded that spiritual truth is embodied publicly in the Scriptures, understood according to the sense of the core of Christian faith arising from reading the Scriptures themselves. It was a framework within which all the many profiles and teachings and events of the Scriptures hung together to make sense as a coherent story of God's salvation. He called this "the rule of faith," or "the rule of truth." For Christians, since the coming of Christ, Scripture is read in a new way. For Irenaeus, Christ is the treasure hidden in the field of the Scriptures, which could not be

---

1. *Constitution on the Sacred Liturgy* (*Sacrosanctum Concilium*), 7 (hereafter, SC.)
2. DV, 13.

fully understood until he came into our world. He threw light on everything written before, like the one missing piece of information that solves the detective mystery. In particular, it is the Cross of Christ that brought about humanity's great moment of Aha! From that point on, Scripture became a treasury of words and images that opens up the mystery of Christ.

For St. Augustine, the tireless reader of Scripture, two centuries after Irenaeus, Christ hides and darts everywhere in the leafy forest of Israel's ancient books and the Church's newer books, either openly and plainly or stealthily and teasingly. Who else but Christ, Augustine asks, was in Isaac carrying his own sacrificial wood, or wrestled Jacob to a draw, or appeared in Joseph's fiery trials, Moses' burning bush, Passover's slain lamb, or on Paul's road to Damascus? Augustine echoed the disciples on the road to Emmaus when he wrote:

> Christ meets and refreshes me everywhere in those Books, everywhere in those Scriptures, both in their open spaces and in their secret hideaways. He sets me on fire with a desire that comes from having no little difficulty finding him. That only makes me more eager to soak in whatever I find, to hide it deep in my bones, and to hold it close for my salvation.[3]

2. We Hear in Scripture an Audible Sacrament

Sacraments mediate to us (that is, provide a bridge) to heavenly and divine things by means of earthly and human things. Bread, wine, oil, and water mediate the divine presence through taste, touch, and smell. Above all, in the Eucharist we receive the Lord Jesus Christ himself, as the Council of Trent taught, "body and blood, soul and divinity." These are not simply static, eternal essences, but rather dynamically active embodiments, teeming with life, of our Lord's entire history from his descent from heaven, through his living, dying, and rising again among us, to his Ascension to God's right

---

3. *Answer to Faustus the Manichean*, 12.27.

hand. Pope St. Leo the Great (fifth century) famously said, "Our Redeemer's visible presence has passed into the sacraments."[4]

So it is with the Scriptures and Catholic reading. Its words are sacraments, for they bring to us the presence of Christ—through the sense of hearing. Augustine once spoke of the pillar of cloud by day and fire by night of the Exodus wilderness journey as signifying God's presence by "visible words." Taking a cue from that, we might speak of reading Scripture as an "audible sacrament." It does not merely point to or recall to our minds the things of God, but brings Christ's presence to us like the sacrament of the altar. "The Church has always venerated the divine Scriptures just as she venerates the body of the Lord, since, especially in the sacred liturgy, she unceasingly receives and offers to the faithful the bread of life from the table both of God's word and of Christ's body."[5] This expresses a very ancient Catholic tradition. The greatest biblical interpreter of the ancient Church, Origen of Alexandria, wrote "You are, therefore, to understand the Scriptures in this way: as the one perfect body of the Word [Christ]."[6] The great biblical master and translator, St. Jerome, (from the fourth and fifth centuries), who had studied Origen closely, wrote that we Christians "nourish ourselves with [Christ's] flesh and drink his blood, not only in the Eucharist but also in reading sacred Scripture. Indeed, true food and true drink is the word of God, which we derive from the Scriptures." Elsewhere even more strongly Jerome declares: "For me, the gospel is the body of Christ. . . . When we approach the Eucharistic mystery if a crumb falls to the ground we are troubled. Yet when we are listening to the word of God, and God's Word and Christ's flesh and blood are being poured into our ears yet we pay no heed, what great peril should we not feel?"[7]

---

4. Sermon 61, on the Ascension.

5. DV, 21.

6. Quoted in Hans Urs von Balthasar, *Origen: Spirit and Fire*, trans. Robert J. Daly, SJ (Washington, DC: The Catholic University of America Press, 1984), no. 156.

7. These quotes from Jerome come from Pope Benedict's *The Word of the Lord Verbum Domini*, 54 and 57, respectively.

3. We Find in Scripture God's Powerful Sacramental Word

A Catholic way of reading Scripture recognizes the forceful sacramental impact of the Word of God. As sacraments, therefore, the words of Scripture are not mere pictures but instruments and channels of divine power. It is a perspective on Scripture that the Church learned from ancient Judaism.

We are accustomed to hearing thousands of words on a daily basis. Most don't actually change anything, but some very special words do not merely *describe*; they also *perform*. Powerful in themselves, they accomplish what they talk about. Think of a king issuing a decree, or a judge pronouncing guilt and innocence, or a couple saying "I do" on their wedding day. Words spoken, lives changed! Similarly, God's Word informs and commands, but also acts.

> Yet just as from the heavens
>> the rain and the snow come down
> And do not return there
>> till they have watered the earth,
>> making it fertile and fruitful,
> Giving seed to the one who sows,
>> and bread to the one who eats,
> So shall my word be
>> that goes forth from my mouth;
> It shall not return to me empty,
>> but shall do what pleases me,
>> achieving the end for which I sent it.
>
> (Isaiah 55:10–11)

God's Word enacts life. The classic picture of God's powerful Word appears in Genesis 1, where God *speaks* creation into being—sun, moon, stars, and earth with all its creatures and vegetation. Notice how the phrasing of the text explicitly highlights God's *Word* as the instrument that creates: "Then God *said*: Let there be light, and there was light . . . " (emphasis added; Genesis 1:3). The same picture of

God, the Creator, reappears in the psalms in songs of awe and wonder: "By the LORD's word the heavens were made; / by the breath of his mouth all their host" (Psalm 33:6). "The voice of the LORD is power; / the voice of the LORD is splendor. / The voice of the LORD cracks the cedars" (Psalm 29:4–5). This same Word was delivered to the prophets. "The lion has roared, / who would not fear? / The Lord GOD has spoken, / who would not prophesy?" (Amos 3:8). "The word of the LORD . . . is as if fire is burning in my heart, / imprisoned in my bones; / I grow weary holding back, / I cannot!" (Jeremiah 20:8–9). Thus for Israel, "It is not by bread alone that people live, but by all that comes forth from the mouth of the LORD" (Deuteronomy 8:3).

In the New Testament we witness the ancient Word of the Lord repeatedly reaching fulfillment. The Lord Jesus strides across the pages of the Gospel accounts, speaking words that are powerful and effective. "He drove out the spirits by a word," notes Matthew, "and cured all the sick, to fulfill what had been said by Isaiah the prophet: 'He took away our infirmities / and bore our diseases'" (Matthew 8:16–17, quoting Isaiah 53:4). Through all four Gospel accounts, Jesus refutes evil, forgives sins, stills storms, heals diseases, and conquers death by his powerful command. Jesus *speaks*, something *happens*, and the evangelists *take note*. "He stretched out his hand, touched him, and said, 'I will do it. Be made clean.' His leprosy was cleansed immediately" (Matthew 8:3). "He woke up, rebuked the wind, and said to the sea, 'Quiet! Be still!' The wind ceased and there was great calm" (Mark 4:39). "Jesus rebuked him and said, 'Be quiet! Come out of him!' Then the demon threw the man down in front of them and came out of him without doing him any harm" (Luke 4:35). "He cried out in a loud voice, 'Lazarus, come out!' The dead man came out" (John 11:43–44). These texts clue us into the forceful Word of Jesus that has passed over into the Scriptures. Catholics reading Scripture venerate a Word that transforms our lives.

4. We Attend to Scripture's Priority for Storytelling

The most important way of first knowing and receiving God's power through the sacrament of Scripture is through its stories. No one knew this better than Augustine. About the year 400, he received a note from a deacon in a neighboring North African congregation, a man named Deogratias, who had lately been very displeased with how he taught inquirers. A great admirer of Augustine's teaching and knowledge of Scripture, he wrote asking for help. How might he keep from boring others and himself by teaching the same basics over and over again? Augustine responded by dictating a fascinating little work, *Instructing Beginners in Faith*, which told Deogratias that repetition matters less than the enthusiasm and humility of the teacher; for the faith of inquirers begins to stir with every retelling of the salvation story. The call of Abraham, the sacrifice of Isaac, the trickery of Jacob, the wisdom of Joseph, the Exodus under Moses, giving the covenant at Mt. Sinai, and David's ascent to the kingship of Israel, Judah's exile in Babylon and eventual restoration, and of course the story of Jesus' birth, life, teaching, Death, Resurrection, and Ascension: the Bible's Big Story, and its many little stories in between, all ignite inquirers by conveying the vast and varied love story between God and humanity.

Deogratias asked, Where do I start and stop? Augustine replied that a complete summary of Scripture's salvation story begins with the first moment of creation and ends with —this morning's Church news! The deacon's eyebrows surely shot straight up. Wait, what? Who can cover all that? With a wink Augustine quickly adds that one need not cover every detail, but should sketch the story's most remarkable events, its "critical turning points." He's referring to the eras from Adam to Noah, from Noah to Abraham, from Abraham to David, from David to the Babylonian captivity, from the captivity to the coming of Christ, and from Christ's coming to the present. Reading, reciting, and knowing that storyline has the power to display

God's love vividly and understandably, not as an abstraction, but as a living reality. Nothing, Augustine wrote, has the power to change our hearts more than a story that tells us we are loved.

Augustine uses quotes from New Testament letters to explain the biblical story. God first loved us (1 John 4:19) and did not spare his only Son, but delivered him up for us all (Romans 8:32). We were still enemies when Christ died for us; he did this to demonstrate God's love (Romans 5:8). He showed that the purpose of the Law is love (1 Timothy 1:5), which Paul calls its "fulfillment" (Romans 13:10). Jesus laid down his life for us, so we should lay down our lives for our brothers and sisters (1 John 3:16). Thus the heart of the Bible is love for God and neighbor fulfilled and given to us by Christ.

Love begins with the embrace of faith: faith's first hesitant steps are the crucial beginning of the journey toward true knowledge of God. The Bible tells us a coherent story of love that leads to an exalted outlook on the world, with majestic ethical principles and examples of lives lived in sacrificial service in the cause of justice and compassion, culminating in the figure of Jesus. All of this combines with a magnificent history of thousands of repentant sinners and striving saints (along with many villains in the Church's story too). On balance this story brings out a deep and often hidden dignity of humanity that is not usually evident in history books or on the nightly news. On that basis we give initial credence to the Bible's central story, and allow its witness to divine love to seep into our hearts. With the opening of the heart and mind by love, a marvelous new world of understanding opens up. (For this reason, the book's introductory approach in part 2 will focus on the Bible's stories. Reading them is the best and most delightful way to learn how to read Scripture.)

The great Swiss theologian Karl Barth, whose books fill entire library shelves, visited America in 1962. A student in Chicago asked him to sum up his life's work in a sentence. He said after a pause,

"Yes, I can, in the words of a song I learned at my mother's knee: 'Jesus loves me this I know, for the Bible tells me so.'" The Bible's stories of that love stir believers to love God and neighbor.

5. We Embrace Scripture's Mysteries

Catholic readers of Scripture fearlessly welcome its mysterious qualities; they let awe and wonder have their rightful place, refusing to reduce Scripture to mere clear ideas and Hallmark-card sentiments. Scripture teaches about God, after all, the most awesome mystery there is, and seeks to lead human beings to know this God in faith. This is not news, but what does it mean? We don't know God the same way that we know a tree or a book or a pencil. God is our *Creator*, and so is unlike *every* other being; knowledge *of God* therefore must also be completely unique. This kind of knowledge develops differently than any other kind of knowledge we have: it is knowledge based in mystery. But let's not be fooled by the word "mystery." Because religious people speak about things that cannot be understood in the usual ways, some think the word "mystery" checks our minds at the door of reason, and pampers religious people who don't know how the real world works. (Some people think science can explain everything, that any minute now science will provide life's ultimate explanations. But many more sober thinkers say that that is beyond the reach of true science.)

However, the Catholic sense of mystery, which has no quarrel with science, believes that "mystery" refers to something that we *can* understand—but cannot exhaust. It is a different sort of knowledge than the kind we seek every day to manipulate our world. This knowledge walks the shoreline and wades in the shallows of divine mystery's vast ocean. Some expert voyagers have the know-how to launch out into deep mystical knowledge, but even they never touch the bottom of the mystery of God. The power of reason is effective *as far as it goes*, but remains insufficient to achieve full understanding. That means that learning about God from a Catholic reading of

Scripture is an adventure that includes but goes beyond ordinary ways of knowing by relying on the Holy Spirit and faith. So the Fathers of the Second Vatican Council affirmed that in Scripture God chose to share "those divine treasures which totally transcend the understanding of the human mind."[8] And this is a marvelous thing! As St. Gregory of Nyssa pointed out in the fourth century, that God is infinite means that we can expect to work joyously *forever and ever* at our task of loving and learning about God. For now, Scripture gives us strong tastes of that love and learning, so by believing and loving we have already begun our eternal life with God. This means that the Catholic reading of Scripture finds its native habitat in an attitude of prayer and devotion. For this reason the Mass, which replicates the worship of the heavenly beings, is the setting par excellence for reading Scripture. This is particularly true of the Gospel reading, set between two burning candles that signify God's presence.

Because Scripture conveys an untamable God, it reflects something of God's untamable mystery. The great third-century Scripture interpreter, Origen of Alexandria, saw that the hidden mysteries of Scripture were like those that the scientists of his day were seeking to uncover and explain. Fast forward to the nineteenth century, not many years after Lewis and Clark's wilderness expedition in the American Northwest, when the Englishman John Henry Cardinal Newman (beatified in 2010) compared the Bible to a vast uncharted territory.

> [Scripture] cannot, as it were, be mapped, or its contents catalogued; but after all our diligence, to the end of our lives and to the end of the Church, it must be an unexplored and unsubdued land, with heights and valleys, forests and streams, on the right and left of our path and close about us, full of concealed wonders and choice treasures.[9]

---

8. DV, 6.
9. *An Essay on the Development of Christian Doctrine* (1845) I:14.6.

Catholic readers accept Scripture's mysterious wildness while blazing trails through its forests and valleys as far as God will allow, knowing that their deep recesses offer untold nourishment.

6. We Study Scripture's Human Dimension of History and Literature

Just as the Word became flesh and, despite sharing all our limitations and weaknesses, revealed God to us, so God communicates his saving message of creation, redemption, and re-creation through Christ by using human events and human words. That's why all the dynamics of history, language, and literature come into play to understanding these texts, and help us discover the Word of God. Because of their humanness, we study the texts, at least initially, using ordinary human methods of analysis and the ordinary ways that people learn. Using the same skills we learned as children in reading books, we imagine events as the words convey them to us; we enjoy the beauty of poetry and the artistry of storytelling. The technical way of putting this is to say that Catholic readers respect *the historical and literary dimensions of the text*. Once again the Second Vatican Council's *Constitution on Divine Revelation* makes the point well (emphasis added):

> The interpreter must investigate what *meaning the sacred writer intended to express and actually expressed* in particular circumstances by using *contemporary literary forms* in accordance with the situation of *his own time and culture.*

> For the correct understanding of what the sacred author wanted to assert, due attention must be paid to the *customary and characteristic styles of feeling, speaking and narrating which prevailed at the time of the sacred writer,* and to the *patterns men normally employed* at that period in their everyday dealings with one another.[10]

---

10. DV, 7, 12.

I'll expand on these points in chapter 3, "Getting Grounded: How Catholics Read Scripture in the Twenty-First Century."

7. We Read Scripture "for the Sake of Salvation"

The *Constitution on Divine Revelation* makes a further point: "The books of Scripture must be acknowledged as teaching solidly, faithfully and without error that truth which God wanted put into sacred writings *for the sake of salvation.*"[11] The point would seem obvious, but it embeds something crucial: Scripture's purpose is not to make definitive pronouncements about science or medicine or warfare or human development. Its main focus is God's Word *for salvation.* A Catholic reading of Scripture aims to interpret the Word of God according to that purpose, even if other frameworks are assumed by the writers themselves. For example, one must not read Genesis 1 for scientific knowledge about the structure of the universe. It simply does not give information about science, cosmology, or physics, not even in some hidden esoteric way. One must read according to Scripture's overall intent, which is to bring salvation. This does not mean that we cannot interrogate the texts to discover what the ancients believed about science, languages, education, medicine, and the thousand other things that modern people want to know about. But we should be clear that such questions read against the grain and beside the point of the text's concern (which gave rise to the text in the first place) to speak about our relationship to God. Ancient writers should not be held accountable for not knowing modern scientific ideas; and we are not allowed to think that just because God is all-knowing and Scripture's ultimate author, modern scientific truth lurks beneath the primitive ideas' forms. No. God's choice to accommodate his Word to human languages and cultures ensures that ancient people were allowed to work with the concepts and patterns

---

11. DV, 11.

of writing that they knew. God was willing to risk submitting the precious message of eternal salvation to *changeable* human ways of thinking, speaking, and acting!

This attitude not only frees ancient authors from accountability for not holding modern views; it frees us modern readers to use perspectives and tools that are natural to us in order to investigate the texts. It also frees us from what C. S. Lewis called "chronological provincialism"—the arrogance of judging past people by one's own standards—just as later generations looking back will hopefully not judge us by theirs. That also breeds in all readers a teachable humility that allows past "primitive" peoples like those of the Bible to become our judges in matters of the spirit. This humility is an excellent component of a Catholic reading of Scripture. It discovers that ancient people were more astute about matters of the heart and soul than our often spiritually dunderheaded modern world.

8. We Hold Scripture's Fruitful Tension-in-Unity

The key to understanding Scripture's remarkable dexterity and suppleness, as well as the interactive fruitfulness of all its elements, is the principle of sacramentality. This gathers up aspects I've already mentioned, beginning with the analogy to the seamless union of full divinity and full humanity in Jesus Christ. Thus a Catholic reading of Scripture is humanly and historically grounded without losing its divinely spiritual verve; it honors emotional depth without losing intellectual acuteness; it breeds a sense of personal spiritual freedom without shirking responsibility for others in loving and just relationships; it stresses tradition and discipline without losing spontaneity and delight. It is conservative and yet daring, ancient and yet new; strong and yet tender; globally-focused and yet locally-oriented; conscious of the community and yet aware of the individual. The Lord himself mediates everything and stands as the model for Scripture's marvelous fruitful tension; as the Letter to the Colossians memorably put it, "in him all things hold together" (1:17).

The Catholic reading of Scripture maintains a lively balance that brings together many perspectives in a fruitful tension—historical, literary, liturgical, theological, moral, mystical. Less grounded approaches that turn up in a Google search lack this good tension. One perhaps misses the kick and spark of finding that exact text that speaks to the immediate need of the moment. Catholic reading is a slow, deliberative affair, whose fruitfulness comes less in single bursts and more in patient cultivation. Over time one learns by experience how deeply biblical the Catholic outlook really is, one that through the ages has unfolded from Scripture naturally, fully, and majestically, like the acorn that has become a great oak tree.

Catholic readers of Scripture with the oak tree outlook discover the Bible to be *a single book with many complementary aspects.* Though, with many literary forms, and written over many centuries, Scripture is one bound Book, glued into a single volume by the charity that comes from Christ. Its wild variety of stories, laws, prayers, doctrines, characters, rituals, and practices all interconnect and interact and interpret each other. Persistent readers soon find patterns that unite and cross-fertilize the diverse elements. The most important dimension of this one-Book unity is the interrelationship between the Old and New Testaments. As St. Augustine said, "the New is in the Old concealed, and the Old is in the New revealed."[12]

To describe this scriptural unity, St. Irenaeus proposed the image of a mosaic—little colored stones artfully arranged—that forms the image of a King, who is our Lord. This mosaic metaphor further illustrates his "rule of faith" (mentioned earlier) wherein all the little details of the Bible align to reveal the coherent story of God's salvation. Just as the mosaic's many pieces form a picture of the Lord, so Scripture's many details—all the ancient stories about creation, the patriarchs, the Exodus, the giving of the covenant at Mt. Sinai,

---

12. *Questions on the Heptateuch*, 2.73.

the kingship of David, the preaching of the prophets, the Wisdom literature, and the visions of the apocalyptic writers—reveal a picture of Christ to the reader. Ultimately he is their center and interpretive key. Different people at various times—in Irenaeus' time it was a fluid movement called Gnosticism—select Scriptures to fashion the Christ they are looking for. They rearrange the tiles into an image of a dog or fox, says Irenaeus, and then claim it is the King.

> They disregard the order and connection of the Scriptures, and as much as in them lies, they disjoint the members of the Truth. They transfer passages and rearrange them; and making one thing out of another they deceive many by the badly composed fantasy of the Lord's words that they adapt.[13]

It is a very human tendency to start with one's own ideas, to clothe them in the words of Scripture, and then think that they portray Christ. The holistic Catholic approach to reading Scripture uses the outline of faith, "the rule of truth"—the Creed we recite every week is one form of it—that protects against this.

This Catholic approach to reading Scripture feeds many spiritual practices of the Church: theology, morals, liturgy, spirituality, and cares for the needs of individual readers. This suggests its amazing fruitfulness. Furthermore, because God's Word transcends the human times and cultures that first produced the texts, it interacts with many different cultures and people across the generations to produce new understandings. Catholic readings of Scripture refresh individual readers and the whole Church in ever-new ways, day after day, year after year, age after age. New insights continually emerge from the interaction between the Church's tradition of reading and new human situations. True and authentic new interpretation and understanding of the Word of God occurs in liturgy, prayer, religious and lay pastoral service, private and group study, ecumenical and interfaith conversations, and in many more settings.

---

13. *Against Heresies* I, 8, 1; trans. Unger and Dillon.

This sheds light on Scripture's sometimes puzzling diversity of viewpoints. The Scriptures often put opposing viewpoints side by side, as if to give all voices a right to be heard, even if the perspectives are not only different, but contradict each other. For example, we have two clearly complementary accounts of creation in Genesis 1–2. The transition to kingship in Israel in 1 Samuel 8–12 swings back and forth between pro-king and anti-king viewpoints that may reflect perspectives of the northern and southern kingdoms of Israel and Judah. So which one is right? The biblical storyteller might respond with a wink to that question, "Yes." Both are true in their own way, and the Bible is perfectly comfortable including both. We see this in the self-critique of the Wisdom traditions of the Bible, where the Books of Job and Ecclesiastes question views that are basic to the Book of Proverbs. The New Testament has not one but four Gospel accounts that overlap at many points but also contain details that cannot be reconciled. There are other examples.

This is important for understanding the Bible's true character. The Fathers of the Second Vatican Council pointed out that the Old Testament teaches "some things which are incomplete and temporary."[14] (For example, the Old Testament only hints at the resurrection of the body, and lacks a strong sense of eternal life.) Nevertheless it remains "permanently valuable" as "the true word of God." The key, the Fathers go on, is that we should read Scripture with a sense of its unity which reveals its "true divine pedagogy."

The Bible is not a mere answer book; we don't just open it randomly for magical direction, like a Ouija board, and we don't just look up answers in it, as in the back of a book of crossword puzzles. That puts the onus on us to discover Scripture's deeper unity beneath its conflicting passages. But as with Jesus' parables, the Bible doesn't hand truth to us on a platter; it demands work and thought and practice. This puts in context some difficult passages like the war imagery in Joshua or Revelation, the violent cursing in Psalms 109 and 137,

---

14. DV, 14–15.

the disparaging views of Jews in John 8 and 1 Thessalonians 2, or the problematic views of women in Ezekiel 23 and 1 Corinthians 11. The Catholic reading of Scripture allows these difficult passages to stand, because it understands that Scripture's larger message balances, or even reverses, their claims.

9. We Read Scripture in Community

The Catholic reader of Scripture recognizes that God saves us in a community. Yes, Jesus is a "personal savior": he personally healed people one by one rather than en masse, as when he healed the poor leper with a personal touch. But notice that he then sent the healed man to give testimony to the local priest and to make an offering that would restore him to his family and community (Mark 1:40–44). Jesus saves persons by incorporating each one into his community, something symbolized by the countless meals that he ate with sinners, the self-righteous, and the poor. St. Paul thought not in terms of individuals only, but of the Church; that was the basis of his counsel to the difficult and individualistic Corinthians in the two letters he wrote to them. Look, he told them, "in one Spirit *we were all* baptized into one body, whether Jews or Greeks, slaves are free persons, and *we were all* given to drink of one Spirit" (1 Corinthians 12:13).

A Catholic reading of Scripture, even in the privacy of personal prayer, reads with a spiritual community. Scripture belongs to the entire Church, past and present, and we read the texts with all believers, implicitly or explicitly, while relying on the same Holy Spirit and believing in the same Lord. Thus the whole Communion of Saints plays a role in the work of reading Scripture well. That's why a Catholic reading of Scripture tends to back away from the outlook of the great Harvard scholar of psychology and religion, William James (1842–1910), who defined religion as "the feelings, acts, and experiences of individual men in their solitude."[15] Likewise, it winces at the idealization of a person reading alone as the most authentic and

---

15. *Varieties of Religious Experience* (1902), Lecture II.

fruitful way of reading Scripture, and of "Scripture alone" as the only source of spiritual understanding. Of course personal Bible reading is valuable, but the Catholic paradigm of reading Scripture tends to think rather of people, whether alone or together, reading in spiritual communion with the Church. That grounds the Church's important sense of Catholic tradition as a constant guide to reading. "Consequently it is not from Sacred Scripture alone that the Church draws her certainty about everything which has been revealed. Therefore both sacred tradition and Sacred Scripture are to be accepted and venerated with the same sense of loyalty and reverence."[16] That is, we all (including readers of ages past) hold different keys to Scripture's closed doors, and so must open those doors for one another. We spark each other to ask, seek, and knock, so that each may receive, find, and discover open doors (see Matthew 7:7–8).

St. Augustine, sitting in his bishop's chair (the position for teachers in the ancient world) told his congregation:

> What do I desire? What am I longing for? Why am I speaking? Why am I sitting here? What do I live for, if not with this intention that we should all live together with Christ? That is my desire, that's my honor, that's my most treasured possession, that's my joy, that's my pride and glory . . . *I don't want to be saved without you.*[17]

Augustine's sensibility here grows from a sense of Catholic community according to a somewhat novel conception that he called "the whole Christ" (Latin, *totus Christus*). Grounded in the teaching of St. Paul about the Church as Christ's Body (see 1 Corinthians 12:12–27), and developed by reading the work of a man named Tyconius, Augustine discerned Christ and the Church as a single person in one body. The Lord our head and we his members are so united in spirit and in love that each can speak in the name and even with the identity of the other. The bond of love between the head and the body is like that between spouses joined to each other forever as "one flesh"

---

16. DV, 9.
17. Sermon 17.2.

(drawing on Genesis 2:24). Augustine liked to say, "If two in one flesh, why not two in one voice?"[18] That is to say, the words of Scripture being Christ's Word (particularly, for Augustine, in the Psalms), Christ's Word in Scripture is also our word, and our word is Christ's Word. This "marvelous exchange" is the basis of redemption and the infusion of grace in our hearts that allows God's love to flourish and transform us. It is based on a spirituality of unity between Christ and the Church which has been explored by contemplative writers, from Gregory the Great to Thomas Merton.

For the purpose of the Catholic reading of Scripture, this conception has two aspects, one relating to writing Scripture, the other to reading it. The first is that although Augustine knew that human beings wrote the Bible, those human beings were "members" of Christ (including all the writers of the Old Testament, who were "members–in-waiting"). Thus he could say that through them *Christ himself wrote all the Scriptures*. (This is another aspect of Christ as Scripture's center and unity discussed above.) But the second bears directly on the Catholic reading of Scripture. Because we are members of one another and of Christ we have access together to "the mind of Christ" (1 Corinthians 2:16), and thus by prayer and the discipleship of faith in community we read Scripture together, as it were, with the eyes of Christ himself. In short, it means that we read with a sense of the grace and love that he brought to the world.

Augustine shares a profound insight with St. Athanasius' beautiful little treatise, *Letter to Marcellinus on the Psalms*. Because we belong to Christ, we are able to project ourselves into the texts, that is, to feel that *these are our texts*, they speak *our words*, as if we ourselves or people we know in our community had composed them. This identification is especially dramatic when reading texts like the Psalms, where Catholic tradition from the earliest centuries has seen Christ as the speaker. We read these texts not by simply identifying with the human emotion or events going on in them (though that too

18. *Exposition of Psalm* 142.3.

is important). We read their words as our own words because they are Christ's own words: because they are Christ's words, and we belong to Christ, the words also belong to us. Our own voice sounds back to us and reflects mirror images of ourselves back at us. The personal dimension in this kind of reading is therefore very deep—and also deeply communal.

10. We Climb Scripture's Summit in Love

The concluding theme of a Catholic approach to Scripture has been suggested several times above, but deserves its own statement: it concerns *love*. This is the Holy Grail of the Bible, the theme to which all things lead and from which all things flow out; in Scripture's vast forest, love is the nourishment lying in plain sight in every open meadow or hiding in every leafy patch of shade.

Augustine picked up this sense of Scripture's unity by focusing on the interactive unity wrought by Christ and the love that he brought from God to our hearts through his own sacred humanity. For Augustine, the whole Bible hangs together, with interlocking parts working together to reveal Christ and divine love to us. Christ's coming displayed and disseminated his love that fulfilled the law of love toward God and neighbor. Union with him plants in us the love that fulfills that law of love. This is why we read, this is what we find everywhere in Scripture, and this is the effect of reading upon us.

One of the loveliest passages about Scripture in all of Augustine's writings appears in *On Instructing Beginners in Faith* (4.8). He is explaining that the double command to love God and neighbor, found in Israel's Scriptures (Deuteronomy 6:5 and Leviticus 19:18), and reasserted by Jesus (Matthew 22:37–40), is the center point of the Bible. I break down the passage here to tease out the process of how Catholics read Scripture. Augustine's key phrase linking Christ and love is italicized in the very middle. Augustine wrote:

1. IF: It's true that Christ came so that people might learn how much God loves them; such that
   a. they might love the One who first loved them; and
   b. they might love their neighbor by the strength of him who commanded them to love and gave his example of love.
2. AND IF: It's true that by reading we discover Scripture's purpose; namely, that
   a. all divine Scripture written down before Christ came was written for the distinct purpose of announcing his coming (he's referring to the Old Testament); and
   b. everything committed to writing and confirmed by divine authority after he came *tells of Christ and counsels love* (he's referring to the New Testament) . . .
3. THEN: We know that upon the two precepts of love for God and neighbor hangs
   a. the Law and Prophets (still the only Sacred Scriptures when our Lord spoke),
   b. and the other "books with divine lettering" later set apart for our salvation and handed down to us.
4. THEREFORE: We conclude (about Scripture's unity based in Christ and love) that *the Old Testament secretly hides the New, and the New Testament shows forth the Old.*[19]

Love, sharply defined by God's utter love for Israel and Christ's love for all, is Scripture's summit. Augustine in fact once called it Scripture's *summa* ("peak" and "summary").[20] But elsewhere he had a more catchy way of putting it: "Love," he wrote, "and do what you want."[21] That is, the human heart healed by God's love is utterly free, for everything it does in love is willed by God.

For the Catholic reader of Scripture, therefore, love in the heart formed by God is

- the goal of God's ancient covenant with Israel;
- the purpose of Christ's coming;
- the effect of Christ's Death and Resurrection leading to eternal life;

---

19. *On Instructing Beginners in Faith,* 4.8.
20. *On Christian Teaching,* 1.35.39.
21. Homily 7 on 1 John, 8.

- the load-bearing beam of the Catholic reading of Scripture, which reveals God's will either plainly and directly (Matthew 22:37–40) or hidden in the myriad stories, characters, rites, events, and laws that train readers to find it and practice it; and
- the high point of the reader's formation, the attitude that can recognize the truth of Scripture, for only the one who loves well, reads well.

CHAPTER 3

Getting Grounded: How Catholics Read Scripture in the Twenty-First Century

From ancient times, interpreters have taught that Scripture's authors were not passive instruments when writing Scripture, and that God used real people to accommodate his Word to our human understanding. But modern perspectives on science and history have opened up new depths of this truth and led to a huge and complex body of reflection that can only be drastically simplified here. In a nutshell it is this: we gain a tremendous amount of new insight, as well as wider access to God's truth in Scripture, by reading the texts with an awareness that *God's word comes to us through human words.*

The Catholic Approach to Reading Scripture Develops over Time

Ancient readers were aware of these issues created by their strong conviction that God had spoken through the sacred authors and their texts. But we are more aware than ever of the chasms of time, thought, and culture that separate us from the communities that first produced the Scriptures. Faith recognizes that somewhere deeply embedded in history and in Scripture's human dimension is an enduring divine message that is relevant for our world. How do we find that?

The Church has always valued human learning at its best as an access point to divine truth. But the rise of science brought a perspective on learning that sometimes antagonized religious pursuits. The Church's early relationship with modern science was rocky, and—to say the least—not well managed (the persecution of Galileo being a case in point). Clearly the Church felt threatened by the new views. Despite this, new scientific methods for learning seemed convincing to more and more people, even inside the Church. This extended to new scientific methods for studying the Bible when they arose in the nineteenth century. At first the Church warily and only hesitantly acknowledged their insights. Many readers of the Bible of the time, Catholics included, were suspicious that historical critics carried an antireligious ideology (something that so-called fundamentalists, and some others, suspect to this day). The Church was extremely cool to the historical-critical method when it first arose.

Over time, resistance lessened as the method's successes stimulated faith indirectly by stripping away layers of misunderstanding and bias, and by uncovering the original dynamism of the biblical texts. The effect was not unlike cleaning the grime of smoke and dirt from an old painting and restoring its vividly beautiful lines and colors. After undergoing this historical treatment, the Bible began to emerge in a new guise that enhanced faith and sparked new love. So the new method worked its way into alliance with religious readers. Especially after Pope Pius XII's guarded approval of modern methods in his 1943 encyclical *On the Most Opportune Way to Promote Biblical Studies* (*Divino Afflante Spiritu*), Catholic analysts began to use historical perspectives to freshen their understanding of the ancient texts.

A turning point came in the mid-1960s when the Pontifical Biblical Commission published its landmark *Instruction on the Historical Truth of the Gospels* (1964). This important document welcomed historical insights about the development of traditions behind the Gospel accounts about Jesus, and went beyond the decreasingly credible claim that eyewitnesses produced them. The Commission affirmed three stages in the development of the Jesus tradition in the first century: first, the events of Jesus' birth, life, Death, and Resurrection; second, the oral preaching of the Apostles and their oral transmission in Christian communities; and third, the compiling, editing, and reshaping of the traditions in the written Gospel accounts. The following year the Second Vatican Council's *Dei Verbum* extended the historical perspective of the previous year's *Instruction* to include the entire Bible.

The tipping point for the gradual Catholic approval of these methods came with the wide acceptance of the analogy made in *Dei Verbum* between Scripture's historical makeup, recoverable using scientific methods, and the human Incarnation of our Lord.[1] As God's divine Word took on human flesh, with all its limitations and weaknesses, to become the mediator between God and humanity, so Scripture's fully human reality (including dependence on human language) mediates God's presence and will to us. Though divine and human dimensions are different, they remain united, complementary, and mutually interpreting. Eventually the analogy to Christ's Incarnation led to a further realization—that the Catholic reading of Scripture is like receiving a sacrament, a feature elaborated in Pope Benedict's XVI's *The Word of the Lord*.[2] As divinity joins inseparably with humanity in the Person of our Lord Jesus Christ, so Scripture, the Church concluded, joins together divine and human to convey divine truth to us. This means that the human dimension of Scripture can be fruitfully studied using the best methods of humanistic learning while not obscuring or blocking the divine. In short, *by God's design, human communication is the basis for divine communication*

A century's worth of progress in scientifically understanding how the Bible works was summarized in the important 1993 document of the Pontifical Biblical Commission, *The Interpretation of the Bible in the Church* (IBC). This path-finding statement, the most extensive of its kind from the Roman Catholic Church, and widely praised both inside and outside the Church, is a clear and judicious

---

1.   This analogy appeared in DV, 13: "Indeed the words of God, expressed in human language, are in every way like human speech, just as the Word of the eternal Father, when he took on himself the weak flesh of human beings, became like them."

2.   Sections 52–56.

analysis of Catholic biblical interpretation in the modern world.
Particularly notable is its embrace
and reframing of the historical-
critical method of reading biblical
texts. (The method is actually a group
of interrelated methods and
approaches that emphasize natural human processes by which literature, such as the Bible, is produced.) It's important to understand
that the words "critical" and "criticism" are not in themselves nega-
tive; coming from a Greek word that means "judgment," they point to
a process that may be called "scientific." In this context biblical *criticism* is a rational procedure that spells out the steps involved in the
human creation and development of the texts. IBC lays out the process in exacting detail.

As God's divine Word took on human flesh, so Scripture's fully human reality mediates God's presence and will to us.

Historical-critical methods seek to understand biblical texts by
using scientific approaches that initially lay aside the divine dimension for the sake of understanding the human one. That requires, at
least initially, treating them as purely human creations developed by
natural processes of human communication, and studying them like
any other literary text. This method has underscored the awkward-
ness of the Bible's lack of overall stylistic unity, choppiness of combined sources, discrepancies between earlier views and later
corrections, reflections of cultural prejudices, and other difficulties.
The process reconstructs the history of a written work's production,
like uncovering the steps in the creation of a famous artist's finished
masterpiece, such as first drawings or repainted portions or even
mistakes. Some early historical critics too easily fixated on the component parts of books and reduced their meaning to their sources, as
if the meaning of a painting resided only in preliminary sketches or
paint-mixing techniques and not the finished product on the canvas.
Others went so far as to say the historical method proved the Bible
was *only* human. Even now some scholars find it difficult to believe
that the ancient biblical texts have a saving message for modern

readers. (Usually it is these scholars who end up on talk shows.) Some wariness remains about the method. But strengthened by likening Scripture's human dimension to the humanity of Christ (with the blessing of Pope John Paul II and of Joseph Cardinal Ratzinger, the future Pope Benedict XVI), IBC went beyond affirming the method to insisting on it. "The historical-critical method," it declared, "is the indispensable method for the scientific study of the meaning of ancient texts." Having been composed by human authors, it continued, the proper understanding of God's word "not only admits the use of this method but actually requires it."[3] The Church had come a long way to write those sentences.

How the Rise of Science Has Changed the Way We Read the Bible

Once upon a time, all readers took biblical texts at face value, simply accepting their statements about cosmology, history, and the reports of words and deeds; for instance, Moses physically wrote the first five books of the Bible, and Jesus spoke the Sermon on the Mount exactly as you see it in Matthew 5–7. But that view is no longer possible, for historical-critical analysis has revealed the complexity of the process of witnessing, storytelling, teaching, writing, and transmitting traditions among people and communities. The Church now acknowledges that all these texts passed through many stages of composition and reediting that sometimes reshaped the tradition to fit new needs and ideas.

Consider the biblical story of creation. Genesis 1 frames the story as God's week of work ending with a Sabbath. Genesis 2 then tells of a grown man created from dirt, a grown woman fashioned from the man's rib, and a garden where trees give knowledge, a snake talks, and God walks. At one time the Church accepted the tradition that Moses wrote these chapters under divine inspiration that

---

3.   IBC, I.A.

revealed hidden facts to him. As recently as the 1640s it was still intellectually credible at Cambridge University to assert from the study of Genesis that God created the world in about 4000 BC. People believed that six-hundred-year-old Noah built an ark that survived a worldwide flood; that six hundred thousand people wandered in the desert for forty years after the Exodus; that Jonah sat inside a fish for three days; and so on.

In the last four hundred years a revolution in human consciousness has taken place that is symbolized by names like Galileo, Newton, Darwin, and Einstein. It has changed our perceptions of the earth, the cosmos, and life itself. Biblical people once imagined a three-tiered cosmos of heaven above, underworld below, and earth standing on pillars in between, with the stars strung and sun and moon hung by God, like lamps. Today the Hubble telescope reveals that we live in a galaxy with two hundred billion stars. To reach our largest neighbor, the Andromeda Galaxy, light-speed travel—186,000 miles per second—needs *2.3 million years*. And the universe has *one hundred billion galaxies*. The point is not that we are therefore insignificant, or that ancient people were stupid; it's rather that *our perspective has changed*. We can't read Genesis 1–2 the old way any longer, as description of fact. *Something else is going on here.* If the texts remain true, they are true in a different way than as merely conveying facts. (The case is different when the salvation that the Scriptures intend to convey is tied to factual events, as with Jesus' Death and Resurrection. As the *Constitution on Divine Revelation* says, the Gospel writers exercised certain editing and writing liberties in the way they told their stories, but "always in such a fashion that they told us the honest truth about Jesus."[4])

Close study of the texts using historical-critical approaches has revealed their literary and theological purpose.

---

4. DV, 19.

Close study of the texts using historical-critical approaches has revealed their literary and theological purpose. Different Israelite communities living centuries apart and writing with different reasons and perspectives told two different creation stories. Some feel a sense of loss in knowing this. But on the positive side, this perspective has sharpened our sense of the Bible's strategies of storytelling and symbolic teaching that were forgotten or dismissed when taken only literally. While disallowing the simple equation of truth with historical fact (that something is true because it happened), this perspective has reinstated the perception of truth that includes the insights from sources like stories, parables, and poetry.

The ancient people knew this instinctively; we do not. But we are learning again that to read well is also to read symbolically. In this new perspective we can see Genesis 1–2 assert a deep communion between a worker who honors the Sabbath and the Creator who rested on the seventh day. We can see the creation of the man teaching our utter dependence on God, whose life-giving breath shows him to be closer than our next sigh. We can see the complete interdependence of humanity when the woman is made from the man when everyone afterward comes from a woman. We learn from a knowledge-giving tree that responsibilities grow out of the gifts we have been given; from a talking snake about the serpentine pitfalls that lie in wait for us; and from God walking about the garden that he's always calling and looking for us. The ancient teacher conveyed religious truths for the sake of salvation with supreme creativity and style—these were *not* mere reported facts. Learning this skill of reading symbolically marvelously improves our reading experience. (Actually, it helps us to catch up with early Christian writers and preachers, who read symbolically quite well; we have a lot to relearn from them.) It is more exciting to read the Bible as a many-layered symbolic text than as a narrative that only tells facts. Like moving from two dimensions to three, we can discern height, breadth, and depth in the spiritual symbolism of the texts—even when actual facts are involved (as they often are). Moreover, the necessity of working at interpretation, instead of passively receiving facts, makes the skill of reading part of the search for God.

IBC also stresses that the quest for true biblical interpretation is grounded in the search for *the literal sense of the text*, the key to which IBC locates in *the author's intention*. This is the starting place for investigating Scripture's basic meaning for readers. A text's literal sense refers first of all to the meaning of its letters (Latin, *litterae*), that is, its plain grammatical meaning. But the concern to discover the literal sense of texts and the intention of the author quickly widens into looking for the historical dynamics that shaped the events described and the concepts expressed. This is no simple matter, because it includes study of the influences that converge in a writer and the dynamics of the situation at the time of writing. Examples of these influences include the author's culture, the standard forms of literature that the author drew on, the contours of the situation being addressed, the needs of the immediate audience, and other factors. The task is further complicated by the fact that biblical texts often carry the fingerprints of many hands. Many texts were communal productions that blended different sources.

The process of critically studying a biblical passage moves through several stages that unfold in a sequence. *Textual criticism* compares groups of ancient manuscripts in order to determine the text's earliest form. *Source criticism* analyzes content by classifying different sources and their relationships within larger composite documents (for example, the first five books of the Bible are often thought to weave together several different accounts). *Form* or *genre criticism* studies different types of writing and asks not only how a literary form affects the content of a story (for example, Jesus' parables have an expected format, just as jokes have a punch line and limericks always rhyme), but also how a story's social function and oral transmission changes it. *Tradition criticism* studies the changes within the stories as they passed through different communities over time. *Redaction* or *editorial criticism* analyzes how the final text emerged in the hands of teachers who were part editors, part transmitters, and part creators; they perhaps enhanced the traditions while putting them into a coherent final form (as when Matthew incorporates Mark, but also tweaks it). The Church affirms that it is in these final stages, when sections of the Bible appear as books, that the Word from God begins to emerge.

Finally, the Church looks for the Word of God that emerges from the process of canonization wherein final versions of individual books are incorporated into the larger collection called "Holy Scripture." *Canonical criticism* analyzes the complete set of books that were used and recognized as authoritative by the Church according to the central claims of faith (that is, according to Irenaeus' "rule of faith"). This faith considers the canon of Scripture to be a product of God's master design, something that gave the texts a degree of spiritual authority that their original authors never envisioned. Individual passages and books took on new meaning, or had their ideas corrected, in the context of the larger whole; readers can discern these changes with the help of faith and the Holy Spirit.

This is especially the case with reading the Old Testament in the light of our Lord's Paschal Mystery, which Catholic readers see as an all-embracing context for a full understanding of ancient Israel's Scriptures that came to be called "Old Testament." Reading through the lens of Christ brings insights that stand alongside the original sense of the texts as Jewish readers have understood them. This process of rereading begins to emerge in the New Testament, with Christian writers and readers who were enthralled by the new perspective wrought by our Lord's advent. When they read the Scriptures of Israel, they saw a treasury of texts explaining Jesus.

To Sum Up:

Roman Catholic scholars, teachers, and general readers of Scripture thus follow an informed and balanced process of interpretation that integrates faith with a plurality of scientific, historical, literary, and theological methods. This integrative approach understands

Scripture while keeping at least five themes in mind: (1) that Scripture's ground and purpose is to stir faith; (2) that the texts, with all their diversity, embody a real if complex unity that is teased out by tradition and theology; (3) that all the texts either directly or indirectly lead to displaying and explaining the Paschal Mystery of our Lord; (4) that salient spiritual wisdom has emerged in the Catholic community's history of reading the texts; and (5) that taken together these elements aim at allowing the ancient writings to impact life today in a process that IBC calls "actualization," that is, interpretation of Scripture for the life of the Church. Actualization focuses on the drama of salvation leading to *faith* and conversion of heart, leading to discipleship in *hope* that breeds joy and steadfastness, and to a communion of *love* that practices prayer and does justice in the world. All this grows from reading the story of salvation in Scripture. As St. Augustine succinctly wrote, Christians retell the story so that people, upon "hearing it may believe, by believing may hope, and by hoping may love" (*On Instructing Beginners in Faith*, 4.8).

This modern Catholic way of reading Scripture embraces historical perspectives while asserting a robust sense of faith that these human documents convey the Word of God. Though not always explicit or repeatedly explained, these themes are embedded and operative in the studies that follow in part 2.

CHAPTER 4

Getting Going in a Catholic Reading of Scripture

Where to start? An obvious place to begin is with your experience of the Scripture at Mass, something that all Catholics share. How much Scripture do you know from the Mass? You might like to try an assignment I give my undergraduate students in the introductory Scripture class at the University of Portland in Oregon. In order to see how the Bible functions for living congregations today, students attend a service of their choice from any Christian or Jewish tradition. (While the university is run by members of the Congregation of Holy Cross, CSC, its student body is mixed, about forty-five percent Catholic.) The students attend services as participant-observers, a concept borrowed from cultural anthropologists who study preindustrial peoples around the world by living among them for a stretch of time. They observe customs close up so that their analytical conclusions can grow organically from the actual life of the people. Students watch to see if the Bible is visible in the service, and if so, how it is displayed. Did people bring their own Bibles? Were they available in the pews? Did people read from smart phones? How many readings were there? What texts were used? They make notes, using some further questions:

> Were the texts read from a printed Bible or a book of extracts? Learn the difference between the Bible, the *Lectionary*, and the *Book of the Gospels*.

> How did people show reverence to the text and to the act of reading (for example, processing, bowing, incensing, and so forth)?

How was the Bible discussed in the homily? Did it refer to the past, or the present, or some combination of the two?

How did the preacher expect those listening to the Bible's message to respond?

How would you describe this congregation's view of the Bible? How would a member explain their view to a visitor?

What role does Scripture seem to play in people's lives outside the service?

Does this congregation think God speaks each word in the Bible and every statement must be taken as absolute fact? Or do they think the Bible says some things poetically, and God is the general inspiration behind the words? How do they tell the difference?

I ask the students to draw conclusions about *how the Bible functions for these worshiping people* and about *what these people believe about the Bible.* They must confirm their insights in an interview with the presiding priest, minister, or rabbi (who is usually surprised and delighted to be asked), and then they submit a written report (but you might talk about your experience with a friend).

Catholic students are often quite surprised by what they observe, by what they've often seen but seldom thought about. For example, one doesn't find a complete Bible in a Catholic service; readings come from the Lectionary, the anthology of texts chosen by the Church. But they realize that, nevertheless, *the Mass bristles with Scripture.* Even aside from the liturgical hymns and the readings, including the sung psalm, the Mass is a mosaic of Bible passages. (See the list on the next page.) This exercise transforms people from passive observers (a Catholic problem, as all will agree) to active participants, a perspective that changes everything. What might you notice anew?

Scripture in the Mass

In the name of the Father, and of the Son, and of the Holy Spirit. (Matthew 28:19)

The grace of our Lord Jesus Christ, and the love of God, and the communion of the Holy Spirit be with you all. (See 2 Corinthians 13:13)

Peace be with you. (John 20:21)

(. . . it will become for us) the bread of life. (John 6:35)

(. . . it will become our) spiritual drink. (1 Corinthians 10:4)

Hosanna in the highest. (Matthew 21:9)

Blessed is he who comes in the name of the Lord. (Psalm 118:26)

Holy, Holy, Holy Lord God of hosts.
Heaven and earth are full of your glory. (See Isaiah 6:3)

This is my Body, which will be given up for you. . . . This is the chalice of my Blood. (See 1 Corinthians 11:23–25)

Our Father, who art in heaven,
hallowed be thy name . . . (See Matthew 6:9–13)

Behold the Lamb of God,
(behold him) who takes away the sins of the world. (See John 1:29)

Blessed are those called to the supper of the Lamb. (See Revelation 19:9)

Peace I leave you, my peace I give you. (John 14:27)

Lord, I am not worthy that you should enter under my roof, but only say the word . . . (See Matthew 8:8)

Go in peace. (Mark 5:34)

The Bible clearly has a quiet but massive presence within our liturgical lives as Catholics; these little quotes that dapple the liturgy and the rituals highlight Scripture's pervasive importance. But these are only chips off something much larger, a small selection of gems set out by the Church each week for display atop the enormous jewelry box that is the Bible. A sense of half-hidden treasure, and an eagerness to help people get more out of it, appears in the many statements on Scripture in the documents of the Second Vatican Council. There we learn of the Church's deep desire that we should open this treasure chest for ourselves, dig deep into its fabulous piles of jewels, and take home as much as we want, for the treasure is inexhaustible.

The treasures of the Bible are to be opened up more lavishly, so that richer fare may be provided for the faithful at the table of God's word.

—*Constitution on the Sacred Liturgy*, 51

The Council Fathers spoke in no uncertain terms of their hope that Catholics great and small would make Scripture their own. Reversing an old image of the Church that paternally discouraged people from Bible reading to protect them from error, the Fathers wrote, "The treasures of the Bible are to be opened up more lavishly, so that richer fare may be provided for the faithful at the table of God's word."[1] Again, "Easy access to Sacred Scripture should be provided for all the Christian faithful."[2]

The Church was constructing pathways into the majestic forest of God's Word so that people at all levels of understanding might enjoy its beauty, learn its wisdom, and find its nourishment. As St. Augustine turns to begin a close reading of Genesis toward the end of his *Confessions*, he offers a Scripture-laced prayer for grace in reading and understanding that fits well the exploration we're undertaking in this book.

---

1. SC, 51.
2. DV, 22.

Yours is the day, yours the night (Psalm 74:16),
a sign from you sends minutes speeding by.
Spare in their fleeting course a space for us
To ponder the hidden wonders of your law (Psalm 119:18):
Shut it not against us as we knock (Matthew 7:7; Luke 11:5–10).
Not in vain have you willed so many pages to be written,
pages deep in shadow, obscure in their secrets.
Not in vain do harts and hinds seek shelter in those woods,
to hide and venture forth,
roam and browse, lie down and ruminate.
Perfect me too, Lord, and reveal those woods to me (Psalm 29:9, Latin).[3]

What follows will help you to explore the heights and valleys of Scripture's mysterious but delightful old growth forest. It will walk you into the open lane of the Bible's basic story line, and point out pathways into various books and basic concepts. The work is meant to be practical and concrete. You can walk at your own pace as the Spirit may "reveal those woods," so that you too may "roam and browse, lie down and ruminate."

---

3.   *Confessions*, XI.2.3, trans. Maria Boulding (London: Vintage, 1998).

Part II

Unfolding Sacred Scripture: Touring the Texts

CHAPTER 5

The Pentateuch: Creation, Source of Gift and Wonder

Read: Genesis 1:1—2:4; Psalms 33, 48, and 104.

Genesis comes first in the Bible, the first of the first five books Jews call Torah, and Greek-speaking Jews called Pentateuch (meaning "five scrolls"). But scholars think that Genesis 1 wasn't written until relatively late, perhaps as late as the sixth century BC, after the Babylonians had invaded Jerusalem, destroyed the Temple, captured the king, and killed many people. They carried off others into exile, hundreds of miles east to Babylon. The Judahites, or as they came to be known, the Jews, lived a ghetto-like existence there. They were exposed to ideas and practices of their captors, including the way Babylonians thought the world was created. So the text may have been created in a crisis. Picture yourself trying to raise children in an alien environment with radically different, even antagonistic, views of how the world and we ourselves were made, and by whom.

Many think Genesis 1 is a Jewish answer to the Babylonian story of creation. In that account, the great goddess Tiamat gives birth to many gods out of chaos. When she decides to return creation to chaos, the gods rebel. Marduk leads a battle in which he kills Tiamat and her son Kingu and splits Tiamat's slain body in two. From the upper half he creates the sky; from the lower half he creates the earth. Then from the blood of the dead god Kingu he fashions a new, savage creature, the human being, to be a servant of the gods. What outlook on the gods and humanity does this account suggest? The gods are powerful, but they're also vicious, jealous, and vengeful.

They are creative and purposeful, but their creation is the product of a spectacular act of violence. Humanity is a mere slave—lowly and despicable. If myths reflect a culture's deepest self-perceptions, then the Babylonian stories offer a perspective on the world that is neither attractive nor hopeful (but might make a great video game).

It's possible that the creation story of Tiamat and Marduk was connected to the celebration of Babylon's new year festival, during which they retold the story. To counter the Babylonian story, the Jewish community, inwardly revolting against the ideas of the alien culture, told its own stories about creation's beginning that reflected Jewish values and beliefs. That's what we get in Genesis 1.

Israel's God is powerful, creative, and purposeful, but creates out of generosity, goodness, and serenity. While the Babylonian account sees creation emerge from the bloodbath of the gods, this God's creation emerges in order and peace; he commands it into existence with the regular rhythm of night and day, and never breaks a sweat. The wondrous harmony of creation, its fruitfulness and trustworthiness,

Israel's God creates out of kindness, generosity, goodness, and serenity.

moves even God to admire its beauty: "God looked at everything he had made, and found it very good" (Genesis 1:31). The contrast with the Babylonian creation story could hardly be greater.

Genesis 1 is a narrative version of Israel's *understanding* about God, the Creator. But other parts of the Bible give us something even deeper: Israel's *feelings of wonder and admiration* about God the Creator. Psalm 33 is a marvelous example of one Israelite's awe and wonder before creation that we can feel. We must rejoice, says the psalmist, and give loud thanks, and sing a new song to God. Why?

> For the LORD's word is upright, . . .
> He loves justice and right . . .
> By the LORD's word the heavens were made,
>   by the breath of his mouth, all their host . . .

Let all the earth fear the LORD.
>
> let all who dwell in the world show him reverence.
>
> For he spoke, and it came to be,
>
> commanded, and it stood in place."

(Psalm 33:4a, 5a, 6, 8, 9)

God's love and care as creator continue even now, so stories about creation's beginning are also about the present. They tell us about the God who continually creates and nurtures everything.

We see this in the panoramic beauty of Psalm 104, which showcases Israel's own powerful mythological language for glorifying the greatness of the Lord. He appears "clothed with majesty and splendor, / robed in light as with a cloak" (1c, 2a). And so the psalmist exults in the display of power at creation:

> You spread out the heavens like a tent,
>
> setting the beams of your chambers upon the waters.
>
> You make the clouds your chariot,
>
> traveling on the wings of the wind . . .
>
> You water the mountains from your chambers;
>
> from the fruit of your labor the earth abounds . . .
>
> You made the moon to mark the seasons,
>
> the sun that knows the hour of its setting . . .
>
> How varied are your works, LORD!
>
> In wisdom you have made them all;
>
> the earth is full of your creatures.

(Psalm 104:2b, 3, 13, 19, 24)

Psalm 148 creates a choral symphony of praise to the Creator using the elements of God's creation: lightning, hail, snow, thick clouds, storm wind, hills, fruit trees, cedars, animals wild and tame, kings of the earth, old and young. The hymn reaches a crescendo:

> Praise the LORD from the heavens,
>
> praise him in the heights.
>
> Praise him all you his angels;
>
> give praise, all you his hosts.
>
> Praise him, sun and moon;
>
> praise him, all shining stars.

Unfolding Sacred Scripture: How Catholics Read the Bible

Praise him, highest heavens,
you waters above the heavens . . .
Let them all praise the LORD's name;
for his name alone is exalted,
His majesty above earth and heaven . . .
Hallelujah!

(Psalm 148:1–4, 13, 14d)

This last word means literally, "Praise the Lord!" It is transliterated in English from Hebrew: hallel means "praise," and Yah is a shortened form of the divine name Yahweh, which appears in our Bibles as LORD (more on this name in the section on Exodus, pages 63–71. Yah often appears in names like Isaiah or Jeremiah). A similar long burst of exultant praise appears in the song of three young worshipers of the Lord, who miraculously (and symbolically) sang praise unharmed in midst of the fires of a Babylonian furnace (Daniel 3:46–90). Hallelujah is, of course, a Hebrew form of the familiar Latin and Catholic exclamation, "Alleluia!"

Our Christian perspective expands the Jewish praise for God, the Creator, to include the Word of God, who was with God in the beginning, and who became flesh in Jesus Christ. The Word was present at creation: "All things came to be through him, and without him nothing came to be" (John 1:3). Other New Testament texts continue this theme. The Letter to the Colossians says of Christ, "In him were created all things in heaven and on earth, visible and invisible, whether thrones or dominions or principalities or powers" (1:16). The Letter to the Hebrews explains that God created the universe through the Son, who carries "the very imprint of his being, and who sustains all things by his mighty word" (1:3). This sense of the majesty of the Son of God as Creator comes from the earliest days of Christianity, when after the Resurrection the Apostles identified him with an exalted figure, "Dame Wisdom," the personification of God's Wisdom (see Proverbs chapter 8 and Sirach chapter 24).

CHAPTER 6

The Pentateuch: Humanity, God's Fragile Masterpiece

Read: Genesis 2:4—3:24 and Psalms 8, 90, and 139.

Returning to Babylon's story of creation, not only were the gods ugly and venomous, they also made human beings into slaves, servile creatures without dignity or hope. Contrast that with the two accounts of humanity's creation in Genesis 1 and 2. Unlike the rest of creation that came into being by God's spoken word, humanity appears as the result of a resolution within God's heart: "Let us make human beings in our image, after our likeness" (Genesis 1:26). The persons fashioned by God take their place on a throne of exalted dignity amidst everything that has been created. The announcement of humanity's creation appears in a verse that echoes with a kind of hushed solemnity, words of wondrous beauty heightened by their poetic conciseness combined with liturgical power:

> God created mankind in his image;
> in the image of God he created them;
> male and female he created them.
>
> (Genesis 1:27)

How dramatically different from degraded beings made by snarling Marduk. Genesis portrays humanity as culminating God's creative activity as a sort of masterpiece. Skeptics might consider the text to be a picture of human self-aggrandizing, but against the Babylonian backdrop, it appears rather to be a guard against human self-degradation. It is certainly the basis of a long tradition of Jewish and later Christian insistence on the need to treat everyone, even the lowly, poor, and forgotten, as carriers of God's own image.

The second account of Genesis 2:7 is different, but complements the first account in Genesis 1:27—and together they form the bedrock of the biblical vision of humanity. But it doesn't look that way at first. Genesis 2:7 reads: "Then the LORD God formed the man out of the dust of the ground"; that is, he uses mud to create "Adam." The name comes from the Hebrew word for "ground," so we might nickname him "Earthling" or "Dust-Man." Doesn't this point to humanity's inferior status, in a way comparable to the Babylonian story? Not exactly. Look at what happens next to "Dust-Man": the Lord God "blew into his nostrils the breath of life, and man became a living being" (2:7). God gives life to the man so powerfully and intimately, with such intense love and care, that it replicates the dignity of human beings portrayed in Genesis 1:27.

Together, the two accounts of our creation form the biblical vision of humanity.

The storyteller also wants to impress upon us that however exalted we are, we're also completely dependent upon God; our very breath of life comes from God. Stop right now as you're reading this: take a long, deep breath. Although we don't think about it much, the very act of breathing is pleasurable; we enjoy feeling cool bursts of oxygen and its little explosions of life into our lungs and bodies. What genius of this religious storyteller and spiritual master to use something so basic about us to teach God's intimate loving kindness, and our absolute dependence upon it. This story does not simply describe how humanity began; it also teaches how humanity survives every day, this day, every hour, billions of us breathing in, moment by moment, the gift of life from our stupendously generous and loving Creator.

The dignity that God bestows upon human beings was a source of profound awe for biblical writers. Psalm 8 captures it beautifully:

O LORD, our Lord,

   how awesome is your name through all the earth! . . .

When I see your heavens, the work of your fingers,

   the moon and stars that you set in place—

What is man that you are mindful of him?

   and a son of man that you care for him?

Yet you have made him less than a god,

   crowned him with glory and honor.

You have given him rule over the works of your hands,

   put all things at his feet.

(Psalm 90:1–4, 10, 12).

The writer of Psalm 139 feels the same awestruck wonder as he turns his gaze upon himself and the yawning deep mystery of being a creature of God. "LORD, you have probed me, you know me," he writes, marveling at the exactness of God's knowledge. "You know when I sit and stand; / you understand my thoughts from afar. . . . Even before a word is on my tongue, / LORD, you know it all" (139:1–4). Then he gasps to remember God is everywhere. "Where can I go from your spirit? / From your presence, where can I flee? / If I ascend to the heavens, you are there; / if I lie down in Sheol, there you are" (7–8). (Sheol was ancient Israel's idea of a place for all the dead, not the same as our idea of hell.) "Such knowledge is too wonderful for me, / far too lofty for me to reach" (6). But then he begins to remember that he was once a tadpole-like embryo. "You formed my inmost being; / you knit me in my mother's womb. . . . My bones are not hidden from you, / When I was being made in secret, / fashioned in the depths of the earth. / Your eyes saw me unformed; / in your book all are written down; / my days were shaped, before one came to be" (13–16). How strange and beautiful these words! Consider meditating on them on your next birthday.

While Psalm 139 staggers to think about the first hours of a person's existence, Psalm 90 is awed by thinking of a person's last hours. Its words purport to be from an old man, as the title says, "a prayer of Moses, the man of God." He is at the same time awed by God and grateful before God. He is sorrowful at life's shortness and pain, and yet knows they offer an opportunity for wisdom.

> Lord, you have been our refuge
> through all generations.
> Before the mountains were born,
> the earth and the world brought forth,
> from eternity to eternity you are God.
> You turn humanity back into dust,
> saying, 'Return, you children of Adam!'
> A thousand years in your eyes
> are merely a day gone by. . . .
> Seventy is the sum of our years,
> or eighty, if we are strong;
> Most of them are toil and sorrow;
> they pass quickly, and we are gone. . . .
> Teach us to count our days aright,
> that we may gain wisdom of heart.
>
> (Psalm 90:1–4, 10, 12).

Get out your calculator and try a thought experiment. If you could choose any age at which to die, what would you choose? Here's your chance: be generous! Say you will live to be 100. Multiply the years by 365 days. Congratulations, you've been awarded 36,500 days. Now, how old are you today? Multiply your current age by 365—can you see where I'm going with this?—then subtract that from 36,500, or whatever figure you gave for your life. That's how many days you now have left. The point is that the past is gone quickly, as the future also will be. All we have are the days that are present, and even these are uncertain. "Teach us to count our days aright, / that we may gain wisdom of heart." Out of the ancient past, the psalmist poses a question: "What are we doing with the few days we have?"

The storyteller of Genesis 2, who may have written as early as the tenth century BC, addresses the issue from a different angle. He (or she: some discern marks of female authorship in the stories) portrays humanity's defection from God in the very midst of Eden's abundance. Many see in the story the marks of a fantasy—but one with a serious point. The story takes us into a mythical realm of time out of time, where God walks, a snake talks, and bodies go about bare and unashamed.

Genesis 2 brilliantly portrays the psychology of desire and guilt.

Yet the dream of continuing to live a perfect human life crashes down around Adam and Eve. Jewish readers have seen in this story a cautionary tale about the tendencies of all human beings; for most Christians it narrates the story about original sin—how it infects us and brings death. Either way it speaks of sin as the cause of human sadness, pain, and deviousness, while it also brilliantly portrays the psychology of desire and guilt.

For the Apostle Paul, we are all threatened by death because of Adam's sin. "All are under the domination of sin, as it is written: 'There is no one just, not one'" (Romans 3:9–10, quoting Psalm 14:3). But Paul's mission is not simply to diagnose humanity's ills; actually he seeks to shine a bright light on the power of Christ's Death over sin. He doesn't think, "Look how bad you people are! God sent Christ to save you, so believe!" Rather, he starts with Christ's Death, and thinks, "If the cure was that drastic, *how bad must the disease have been?*" He writes from the point of view of the cure rather than the illness. The result is that, although "all have sinned and are deprived of the glory of God," nevertheless "they are justified freely by his grace through the redemption in Christ Jesus" (Romans 3:23–24). In the end, "as sin reigned in death, grace also might reign through justification for eternal life through Jesus Christ our Lord" (Romans 5:21). The marvel of Christ's Resurrection has reversed the human condition. "Just as in Adam all die," wrote Paul, "so too in Christ shall all be brought to life" (1 Corinthians 15:22). Although humanity sins, God saw that coming a long time ago and planned the road for humanity's long journey back to its original dignity.

This redemption of humanity leads to the great hymns of praise of the New Testament such as we find in the Letter to the Ephesians. "Blessed be the God and Father of our Lord Jesus Christ, who has blessed us in Christ with every spiritual blessing in the heavens, as he chose us in him, before the foundation of the world, to be holy and without blemish before him [that's where we've come from]. . . . In him we have redemption by his blood, the forgiveness of transgressions, in accord with the riches of his grace that he lavished upon us [that's where we are right now] . . . with the promised holy Spirit, which is the first installment of our inheritance toward redemption as God's possession, to the praise of his glory" [that's where we'll end up] (Ephesians 1:3–4, 7–8, 13–14). The long, twisting story of humanity since the Garden of Eden will then come round at last to its happy conclusion.

How does all this happen? We look next at God's plan for humanity's redemption, and where the story of the Bible really begins to take off.

CHAPTER 7

The Pentateuch: Patriarchs Begin the Long Journey

Read: Genesis 12:1–3 and chapters 15, 17, and 22, also Romans 4.

Chronologically speaking, we should place Abraham in the first half of the second millennium, maybe about 1800 BC. The narrative of salvation in the Bible begins with the story of Abraham, which we'll follow through three passages, Genesis: 12:1–3, 15:6, and 17:5–8. In these we'll find seven important points. Five points involve God's approach to humanity; another relates to humanity's response; and the last one concerns how to name their mutual interaction. Genesis 12:1–3 is the launch point for salvation history in the Bible. (Notice that the patriarch, in the passage below, is first called Abram. His name will change as events unfold.) Here is the first passage.

> The LORD said to Abram: Go forth from your land, your relatives, and from your father's house to a land that I will show you. I will make of you a great nation, and I will bless you; I will make your name great, so that you will be a blessing. I will bless those who bless you and curse those who curse you. All the families of the earth will find blessing in you. (Genesis 12:1–3)

1. *"The LORD said"* recalls the primary connection between heaven and earth is God's Word—the same Word that flung the universe into being, cursed the ground beneath Adam, chastised the killer Cain, caused the

The narrative of salvation begins with the story of Abraham.

floodwaters to recede for Noah, and confused the nations by many languages. God speaks and things happen.

2. *"Go"*: In Abram's journey, God's purpose for creation is emerging (still indistinctly for us readers). Previously, God seemed to be creating a plan bit by bit. He creates Adam, realizes he needs a companion, offers the animals, then creates Eve. God seems not to know where Adam and Eve are after they sin, and seems surprised by Cain's act of murder. At one point, he wonders whether he should have ever made creation (6:6). Then, after the flood, he decides never to do such a thing again. But with Abram, a plan is taking shape.

3. *"To a land"*: Abram's destination—this land—will become crucial to the patriarchs, and central to the storyline throughout Scripture. This is "the Promised Land." The patriarchs live in it, then reluctantly leave it, and long for it in Egypt. Joseph makes his family swear they will bring his bones back to the land. Under Moses the now-enslaved nation leaves Egypt in order to return to the land. Joshua divides it; judges and kings defend it. It is where David builds Jerusalem and where Solomon builds the Temple. Ultimately exiled from the land, the people return triumphantly to rebuild their lives before God in the land. It is the land where Jesus roamed (and probably never left), and the land of the Apostles. For Jews and Christians (and later for Muslims) it was and will always be "the Holy Land."

4. *"Nation"*: God's promise of many descendants, a great progeny, is crucial. The ancient world, including Old Testament Israel, had little sense of personal immortality; having many descendants was like living forever. Ultimately God tells Abraham to count the stars in the night sky: "Just so . . . will your descendants be," God says (15:5). This, of course, refers to the promise to create Israel. The choice of Abraham is the basis for what theologians call Israel's "election." When God chose Abraham, he was electing Israel as his people; forever after they are known as "the Chosen People."

5. *"I will show you . . . I will make of you . . . I will bless you"*: Notice the gracious character of God's many promises, although he is not obliged to act kindly. Nothing suggests that Abraham is

unusually worthy. God acts out of pure goodness and generosity. The design that God has in mind for the good of Abraham ultimately extends to Israel and to all humanity. This unearned favor appears again and again in the Bible; it is central to God's identity. God acts out of love and goodness, referred to in the Old Testament as God's loving kindness, or mercy. The New Testament's name for this unmerited favor is "grace." God's grace saves us when nothing else can (1 Corinthians 15:10); grace moves the Lord Jesus Christ to sacrifice himself for our sin (Romans 5:15); the Spirit of grace (Hebrews 10:29) stirs us toward communion with God and one another.

The first five points taken together represent the picture of God seeking out humanity. God loves, God plans, God speaks, God promises, God acts. This is the movement from heaven to earth. Now we look at the final two points dealing with Abraham's response and the conclusion of their agreement. Now for the second passage.

Abram put his faith in the LORD, who credited it to him as an act of righteousness. (Genesis 15:6)

6. *"Abram put his faith in the LORD."* Corresponding to God's movement from heaven to earth is the human movement from earth to heaven: Abram responds to God's overture by believing. This is the crucial response to God—an embrace of the heart. Not mere consent to an idea, faith leans the whole weight of one's existence upon another. In the Bible, "believing" is a personal act of entering into a relationship, and one's whole life is at stake in what one most truly believes. Like one entering into a marriage agreement, Abraham entrusts God with his whole future. He went, as we say, "all in."

This text was the cornerstone of the Apostle Paul's mission to the Gentiles. For him, Abraham was the model believer for both Jews and Gentiles entering into covenant with God. Romans chapter 4 presents his argument. The story in Genesis shows that Abraham was justified, that is, forgiven of his sins, not by works he had done but by faith (Romans 4:3, 9). Paul points out that righteousness was credited to him before being circumcised, which was a seal of righteousness (4:10). This makes Abraham the father of all who believe (4:11–12). The promise to Abraham came not through Law but through faith (4:13), and "depends on faith, so that it may be a gift" (4:16) from God, "who gives life to the dead and calls into being what does not exist" (4:17). Abraham was "fully convinced that what [God] had promised he was also able to do" (4:21) so his faith was "credited to him as righteousness" (4:22). "It was credited" refers not to Abraham alone, but to all "who believe in the one who raised Jesus our Lord from the dead" (4:24). Here is the third passage.

> I will maintain my covenant between me and you and your descendants after you throughout the ages as an everlasting covenant, to be your God and the God of your descendants after you. (Genesis 17:7)

7. *"Covenant between me and you."* The name for the agreement established between God and Abraham (and all his children to come) is "covenant." Despite some legal aspects, a covenant is more than a legally binding contract. It binds persons in a relationship of mutuality that involves both obligation and respect: a covenant of love. It is impossible to overestimate the importance of this concept of the Bible. The covenant is the standard to which both God and humanity commit themselves. God will establish it with all Israel at Mt. Sinai. Psalms celebrate it. Prophets lament when the people break it, and constantly call them back to it. Jeremiah famously prophesies that God will one day establish "a new covenant" with his people. "I will place my law within them, and write it upon their hearts; I will be their God, and they shall be my people" (Jeremiah 31:33). The covenant promise extends into the heart of Jesus' message. On the night before he died, Jesus gave broken bread as his body, and offered his blood as drink, saying, "This cup is the new covenant in my blood, which will be shed for you" (Luke 22:20). This is the fulfillment of Jeremiah's new covenant, that is, the "New Testament." (Our word "testament" comes from the Latin *testamentum*, which translates the Greek word for "covenant.") According to Paul, the Apostles were

"ministers of a new covenant, not of letter but of spirit, for the letter brings death, but the Spirit gives life" (2 Corinthians 3:6).

Time Line of Major Turning Points of Biblical Salvation History

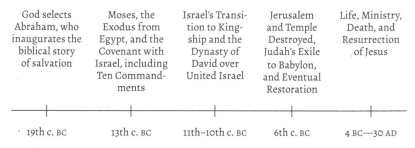

God selects Abraham, who inaugurates the biblical story of salvation	Moses, the Exodus from Egypt, and the Covenant with Israel, including Ten Command-ments	Israel's Transi-tion to King-ship and the Dynasty of David over United Israel	Jerusalem and Temple Destroyed, Judah's Exile to Babylon, and Eventual Restoration	Life, Ministry, Death, and Resurrection of Jesus
19th c. BC	13th c. BC	11th–10th c. BC	6th c. BC	4 BC—30 AD

A lot was riding on this promise to Abraham and his response. It comes, then, as a profound shock when God demands that Abraham sacrifice his son Isaac in Genesis 22. We don't know the origins of this frightening tale, or understand the logic of including it in Abraham's story. It contradicts all we know about the God of the Bible. If God literally wanted this done, it chops off the storyline of the Bible—a short book had Isaac not survived! Why did the story-teller include it? We know that biblical storytellers were not averse to portraying God in ways that seem un-Godlike to us. Genesis did not shy away from picturing God inventing creation as he went along (2:18–19), or not knowing where Adam and Eve were in the garden (3:9), or wishing he had not created humanity at all (6:6–7). Nevertheless, God declares elsewhere that human sacrifice is "some-thing I never commanded nor considered" (Jeremiah 7:31). It boggles the imagination to see God demand of Abraham, not just a human sac-rifice, but the sacrifice of his son specially given by God. The story cer-tainly shows Abraham's utter faith in God. This text is the counterpart to Genesis 15:6, where Abraham "put his faith in the LORD, who cred-ited it to him as an act of righteousness." As noted in the New Testament Letter of James, by his sacrificial act, Abraham "fulfilled" the righteousness that God had credited to his faith (James 2:23).

CHAPTER 8

The Pentateuch: Blockbuster Events of Exodus and Covenant

Read: Exodus 1–3; 34:6–7, Judges 3:7–11, Psalms 30 and 136, and Matthew 14:22–33.

In the Book of Exodus, the saga narrated in the Book of Genesis continues, but now the curtain rises on the greatest story of salvation in the Old Testament. It is so significant that it becomes a wellspring of images of salvation for the rest of the Bible. In fact, as we'll see, the New Testament borrows from it continually to explain the story of salvation through Jesus Christ.

The basic story is quickly told. At the end of Genesis, Joseph's favor with Pharaoh made his whole family secure: his father Jacob, all his brothers and their wives, and their families; "the Hebrews" were prosperous even though displaced from their homeland. (See, for instance, Genesis 47:1–12, where Pharaoh gives generous support to Joseph and his family, and the aged patriarch Jacob "blessed Pharaoh," 47:7). But longing for the land promised to their fathers remains: Joseph's brothers swear to carry his bones back to the Promised Land when they return (Genesis 50:24–25). Many generations pass. Then, suddenly, trouble brews: a new regime arises in Egypt, and the text says ominously, this new Pharaoh "knew nothing of Joseph" (Exodus 1:8). Fear of the Hebrews increases, and favor turns to oppression, including subjection to slave labor. We are told, "The Israelites groaned under their bondage and cried out, and from their bondage their cry for help went up to God. God heard their moaning and God was mindful of his covenant with Abraham, Isaac and Jacob" (Exodus 2:23–24). At that moment, in one of the most crucial chapters of the Bible, a man steps forward who will cast a shadow over the rest of the Old Testament, the New Testament, and beyond in Judaism and Christianity: he is Moses, "the man of God" (Psalm 90:1). In a famous scene, he is tending his flocks on a mountainside when God wondrously appears to him in a flaming bush that does not burn up. God calls to Moses, and makes him the deliverer of his people (Exodus 3:1–15). The great Exodus story has begun.

We'll look closely at two passages in Exodus 3 that are among the richest and most important in the Bible. In the first passage, God tells Moses what he plans to do. "The LORD said: I have witnessed the affliction of my people in Egypt and have heard their cry against their taskmasters, so I know well what they are suffering. Therefore I have come down to rescue them from the power of the Egyptians and lead them up from that land into a good and spacious land, a land flowing

God wondrously appears to Moses in a flaming bush that does not burn up.

with milk and honey" (3:7–8). Then, in an instant, God gives Moses (and through Moses, all Israel) a special revelation of his divine identity. Moses inquires about the name by which Israel may know God. "God replied to Moses: I am who I am. Then he added: This is what you will tell the Israelites: I AM has sent me to you" (3:14).

First Great Teaching of Exodus 3: The Pattern of Salvation

After relative harmony, the descendants of Abraham encounter tragic difficulty and cry out to God, who sends a deliverer that brings them to a new life. This sets up a pattern with five distinct parts: stability, slide into difficulty, outcry to God, act of deliverance, and new stability. This pattern will repeat through the rest of the Bible, including the New Testament, so it's important to understand. Let me summarize briefly what we find in Exodus.

Stage 1: The People in Stability. Jacob's family is preserved from famine in Egypt by the wisdom of Joseph (Genesis chapters 47–50). People find themselves in a situation of relative peace, harmony, or safety.

Stage 2: Israel's Slide into Difficulty. The Egyptians turn against the Israelites and subject them to slavery (Exodus chapter 1). Due to external circumstances or personal fault, a person or the people find themselves entering stormy waters of trouble.

Stage 3: The People's Outcry to God. The people of Israel cry out to God because of their hard labor (Exodus chapters 2–3). The anguish or difficulty causes people or a person to cry out to God.

Stage 4: God Acts to Rescue. God sends Moses to free the people from Egypt (Exodus chapters 3–14). God intervenes in love and power to deliver them; that is, to "redeem" (buy back) or to "save" (rescue) them. This is the root meaning of the common religious words "redemption" and "salvation" (and the titles we give to our Lord, "Redeemer," and "Savior").

Stage 5: Israel's New Stability. Israel is delivered through the Red Sea into freedom (Exodus chapter 15). The people or the person is not merely restored to their earlier state, but brought to a place of new stability.

Keep this pattern in mind, because it reappears in many different contexts throughout the stories of the Bible. Circumstances vary, with different characters and audiences, in texts about entire nations and about individuals. Rescue may be from a physical disease or a political enemy or spiritual guilt. Difficulties may be caused by external circumstances out of the people's control (such as the oppression suffered in Egypt in the Exodus story), or they may be self-inflicted. For example, look at the third chapter of Judges, a book that narrates a series of Israel's defections from God: "Then the Israelites did what was evil in the sight of the LORD; they forgot the LORD, their God, and served the Baals and the Asherahs [fertility gods of the Canaanites], and the anger of the LORD flared up against them. . . . But when the Israelites cried out to the Lord, he raised up a savior for them . . . so the land was at rest for forty years" (3:7–11). One can plot the progress from one stage to the next; you see here stages 2 through 5. In other stories we can see the new stability of peace transforming into an old stability of complacency, and then the pattern repeats. The storyteller's recycling pattern of decline–renewal–decline suggests God's frustration (similar to a distraught parent), and teaches later generations to act differently.

One might use the pattern to plot the story of deliverance embedded in the prayers known as the Psalms—especially the three most plentiful types of psalms, the hymn, the lament, and the thanksgiving. The hymn fits stage 1; the lament fits stages 2 and 3; and the thanksgiving fits stages 4 and 5. In this way, one could treat the psalms as parts of a story, either of individuals or the nation.

Psalm 30 is unique in the way it shows a clear movement through all the stages. Try matching the different verses of the psalm with the different stages. Look at verses 1–6. This is the thanksgiving prayer of an individual who, when unexpectedly facing a severe trial, cried out to God, and eventually experienced a marvelous deliverance. The psalm is his exultant thanksgiving, written at stage 5, looking back in remembrance from his place of new stability. You can see this by noticing the past tenses of the verbs: "I praise you, LORD, for you *raised me up* / and *did not let* my enemies rejoice over me. / O LORD, my God, / I *cried out* to you for help and *you healed* me. / LORD, you *brought* my soul up from Sheol" (30:2–4; emphasis added).

A number of psalms of thanksgiving sound like this. But this psalmist, speaking from stage 5, actually includes in the psalm his past experience of stages 1 through 4. Now look at verses 7 to 12, which reveal his states of mind at each stage. The psalmist once thought his stage 1 stability was his own achievement, but he now sees that that was an illusion. "Complacent, I once said, / 'I shall never be shaken.' / LORD, you showed me favor" (verse 7; stage 1, *stability*). But then came the disorienting slide into difficulty: "But when you hid your face / I was struck with terror" (verse 8; stage 2, *slide into difficulty*). The psalmist never explains exactly what caused that terror, but whatever it was, it was potent and dangerous. He prayed urgently: "To you, LORD, I cried out; / with the Lord I pleaded for mercy: / 'What gain is there from my lifeblood, / from my going down to the grave? / Does dust give you thanks or declare your faithfulness? / Hear, O LORD, have mercy on me; / LORD, be my helper'" (verses 9–11; stage 3, *outcry to God*). Here is the central point of prayer, to call for help from God. We might characterize prayer as the bleat of God's besieged sheep in desperate need. Between verses 11 and 12 we may imagine God's act of salvation appearing, to the psalmist's incredible relief and joy (stage 4, *rescue from God*). Now come serenity and a burst of thanksgiving joy: "You changed my mourning into dancing; / you took off my sackcloth / and clothed me with gladness. / So that my glory may praise you and not be silent. / O LORD, my God, / forever will I give you thanks" (verses 12–13; stage 5, *new stability*). These prayers are meant to model our own situations, and to give us words to pray when we find ourselves in straits. If we pray the words of the psalm in our own situation, in a sense we *become* the psalmist, and the pattern of salvation becomes our pattern too.

The five-stage pattern of salvation, appears also in the New Testament. Consider the familiar story of Jesus walking on water in Matthew 14:22–33. Jesus comes at night to the disciples struggling to row across the Sea of Galilee against a strong headwind. Seeing Jesus moving toward them on the teeming waters, they think he's a ghost. All the Gospel accounts tell this story; but Matthew adds something special and poignant. Take a moment to reread the added scene in verses 28–33, and see if you can discern the stages of the salvation pattern there. Peter dares to say, "Lord, if it is you, command me to come to you on the water." Jesus says, "Come." So Peter gets out of the boat and begins walking on the water toward Jesus; this is a kind of "stability." But seeing the strong wind he becomes frightened, and Peter "slides into difficulty" when he takes his eyes off the Lord. He "cried out" in words that the writer of Psalm 30 would have understood: "Lord, save me!" At that point Jesus "stretched out his hand" to save Peter—stage 4: God acts to rescue. (Compare this with Psalm

136:12, which recalls how the Lord saved Israel from Egypt "with mighty hand and outstretched arm.") Jesus kindly catches Peter, and says, "O you of little faith, why did you doubt?" (Side note: the Greek text of verse 31 shows that Jesus actually speaks a single word, a gently chiding nickname: "O Little-Faith.") At that point the Lord lifts Peter up into the boat, the wind dies down, and the disciples adore Jesus as God's Son in their place of new stability (stage 5). Without question Matthew draws on a salvation pattern that was familiar to him from the ancient Scriptures. People ever after have plugged themselves into Peter's story. Because Peter in a mystical way represents the Church, his cry to Jesus represents the prayer of the Church as a whole and every individual within it. That is to say, Matthew tells Christians the water-walking story through the lens of the ancient biblical pattern of salvation to show that *we are all Peter.*

The New Testament spells out many links between the Exodus story and salvation in Christ. Based on the connection between Christ's Death and Jewish Passover, and the Eucharist as a renewed Passover meal, the Gospels make strong allusions to the Exodus tradition to explain and teach about the meaning of Christ for us. Allusion to the Exodus story appears above all in the title for Christ proclaimed by John the Baptist in John's Gospel (repeated in every celebration of the Eucharist to this day), "Behold, the Lamb of God, who takes away the sin of the world" (John 1:29). Paul uses the Exodus as a model for speaking about Christ's salvation in his letter to the Romans; there he speaks of sin and death as having Pharaoh-like power over our old lives. When the Lord died on the Cross, he wrote, our old self was crucified with him so that "we might no longer be in slavery to sin" (Romans 6:6). He draws out the implications in his first letter to the Corinthians. Because of the Lord's Death we can "clear out the old yeast" of sin and become like bread that is "unleavened" (alluding to the Jewish practice of keeping kosher for Passover). We do this, Paul continues, "for our Paschal lamb, Christ, has been sacrificed" (1 Corinthians 5:7). Elsewhere, Paul makes the Exodus story a model for Christians seeking to remain faithful in their commitment to God (1 Corinthians 10:1–13). The Exodus story is an inexhaustible wellspring of insight into God, Israel, Christ, the Church, the sacraments, salvation—and into Scripture itself.

Second Great Teaching of Exodus 3: The Revelation of God's Name

But this is not all. The Exodus also provides the occasion for God to reveal his personal name to Israel through Moses. Another climactic moment that is important for the rest of the Bible, it rises up majestically alongside the pattern of salvation as a sort of twin peak in Exodus 3.

In the ancient world, names were not mere labels, but embodiments of a person's being; a person's name captured something essential about her or him. When God reveals his name, it is not mere information, but an act of intimacy and love, part of the covenant bond that he entered into with the patriarchs and Israel. God's heavy investment in the covenant included strong affection and devotion, what might be called "covenant love." The Hebrew word *chesed*, difficult to capture in English, is used repeatedly in the Bible to express this boundless covenant love of God. Psalm 136, mentioned above, recalls creation and the Exodus while threading in an antiphonal refrain that sings praise to God "for his *chesed* endures forever." The word is variously translated highlighting one of its many dimensions: *loyalty, faithfulness, mercy, loving kindness, steadfast love*. It points to a devoted love that is not sloppy or temporary, not an emotional flare-up that rages for a while and then dies out. This love burns like a steady blue flame day and night, and stays lit during a windstorm. For that reason, later prophets like Hosea and Jeremiah can compare God's *hesed*-relationship with Israel to a marriage. The passion is strong and steady and vibrant. For this reason, the Bible calls God "jealous" for

When God reveals his name, it is an act of intimacy and love.

his people (Exodus 20:5); this jealousy is not born from self-centered possessiveness, but from beloved-focused and faithful passion.

The name "I AM" is not an abstraction; it is bound up with the faithful love revealed in God's acts of salvation. For ancient Israel's Scriptures, God's identity comes to be known from God's acts: *who God is* becomes known through *what God does*. In a later passage of Exodus that parallels chapter 3, God proclaims his covenant name to Moses in order to encapsulate his character as perfectly loving and just: "The LORD, the LORD, a God gracious and merciful, slow to anger and abounding in love and fidelity [*chesed*], continuing his love [*chesed*] for a thousand generations, and forgiving wickedness, rebellion, and sin; yet not declaring the guilty guiltless . . . " (Exodus 34:6–7).

The name is comprised of four letters in Hebrew, YHWH, and is therefore called the *Tetragrammaton*. It comes from the Hebrew verb "to be" (*hayyeh*), and so suggests that God is the source of all life and being. It occurs almost seven thousand times in the Hebrew Bible, so it is common, and yet it remains mysterious and vaguely threatening. One cannot speak God's name casually, much less blasphemously. The commandment against taking the Lord's name in vain is not a mere nitpick about cussing; it is about revering the reality of the awesome Creator. To speak the divine name was a risky move; it potentially made God's name, and so God himself, vulnerable to misuse or abuse, which was a violation of the covenant (Exodus 20:2). Concern to prevent inadvertent disrespect to the name of God, in fact, stopped Jews from pronouncing it even in the ancient world. By the third century BC, when the Hebrew Scriptures were translated into Greek (in the version called the Septuagint), translators substituted the name "LORD" for the Tetragrammaton. Other sources preferred roundabout ways of speaking of God. The ancient rabbis referred to "the Holy One, blessed be he." A trace of this appears in Matthew's Gospel account, which prefers to speak of "the kingdom of heaven" rather than "the kingdom of God" (as in Mark and Luke). The name YHWH appears nowhere in the New Testament and was not adopted by early Christians. Avoidance of this name continues even today, when most modern Bibles follow the example of the Septuagint by substituting the name "LORD" in small capital letters wherever it appears in the Hebrew text. (An exception is the British Catholic translation, *The New Jerusalem Bible*, which prints the name as "Yahweh." Early English translators used the form "Jehovah," which has fallen into disuse except among Jehovah's Witnesses.)

CHAPTER 9

The History Books: Kingship and Salvation Embedded in the World

Read: 1 Samuel 8–12; 2 Samuel 7, 11–12; Isaiah 2:1–4; 9:1–6; 11:1–7, and Daniel 7:1–14.

After receiving the covenant, the people wandered in the desert for forty years. The texts portray this as a difficult time of apprenticeship, a mixed experience of faithfulness and disobedience with many starts and many stops, few successes and lots of failures. When Moses dies, leadership passes to Joshua; he leads the people across the Jordan River into the Promised Land in a series of military conquests carried out according to the discipline of holy war. This is a difficult history, with much violence and ugly death. Interestingly, modern archaeology does not support the conquest-and-plunder storyline that describes Joshua triumphantly mowing down the Canaanites. Excavations around Jericho, for instance, indicate that the area was uninhabited at the time of the supposed invasion. But the Book of Judges tells a different story; it portrays Israel in constant struggle and negotiation with the people of the land, achieving some victories and suffering many defeats while living among the people.

Even if the stories are inflated, we must ask why ancient storytellers portray Israel and its God as aggressive and merciless toward non-Israelites? Biblical imagery sometimes moves in this direction throughout the Old Testament, especially in its earlier parts, and warrior imagery reappears in the New Testament Book of Revelation. But how does this align with the many other parts of the Bible that portray

God as merciful, slow to anger, and forgiving (Exodus 34:6–7)? Or God being tenderhearted towards his creation, remembering that we are dust (Psalm 103:14)? Or God making a nonviolent covenant with all creation through Noah (Genesis 8:21)? Or God being concerned with all nations of the earth, and guiding them just as he guides Israel (Amos 9:7)? Or God as generous with both the just and the unjust (Matthew 5:45)? Or God as one who shows no partiality (Romans 2:11; 10:12)? Or as God of the Gentiles and not only the Jews (Romans 3:29)? Or God who accepts "in every nation whoever fears him and acts uprightly" (Acts 10:35), who "made from one the whole human race," and in whom we all "live and move and have our being" (Acts 17:26, 28)?

Let's look at just one more text: "God is love" (1 John 4:8). How does this statement sit in the same Bible with the warrior God of Joshua? The answer is that we must prioritize biblical texts; some statements are clearly more significant than others, and determine the meaning of others. The concept of a God who sees all creation as very good (Genesis 1:31), a God who is "gracious and merciful, slow to anger" (Exodus 34:6) and a God who "is" love, *must* trump every other lesser portrayal in order that the full truth of Scripture might be, as Origen said in the third century, "worthy of God." St. Augustine agreed; for him the God who loves and commands us to love God and neighbor wholeheartedly is the same God who gave us the

We must prioritize biblical texts; some statements determine the meaning of others.

Bible to build up that love in its readers. Therefore, he wrote, any text that does not build up this love of God and neighbor must be understood figuratively.[1] And since Christ came to show us God's love so that we ourselves may love God and neighbor as God loves us, then we know that every text of the Bible read rightly either "tells of Christ or counsels love."[2]

---

1. *On Christian Teaching*, 3.10.14.
2. *On Instructing Beginners in Faith*, 4.8.

The Bible often reinterprets itself in order to adjust its teaching to newer priorities and deeper truths. To take only a few prominent examples: God once was said to punish children for their parents' sins (Exodus 34:7), but later, when some wanted to blame parents for their own sins, Scripture says, "only the one who sins shall die" (Ezekiel 18:20). Elsewhere it says that God incited David to disobedience (2 Samuel 24:1), but in the later renarration of the same story in 1 Chronicles 21:1, Satan did it!

Something similar occurs in the story of the transition to kingship in Israel. For two hundred years after entering the land, Israel had no king. The people lived in a loose confederation of the tribes led by chieftains that the Bible calls "judges." But we are not to picture black-robed types administering blindfolded justice. Figures like Gideon and Samson were charismatic leaders with political, military, and religious status who appeared from time to time as needed to defend the tribes from marauding neighbors. Finally the people told Samuel, the last and greatest of the judges, that the time had come for Israel to have a king like other nations. This was a traumatic shift from the loose confederation of tribes, for whom the Lord alone was Israel's king, to a human king. Many people, including Samuel, were anti-king, while others were pro-king. Both sides told stories to promote and justify their points of view. Both sides contributed to the story of how kingship developed in 1 Samuel 8–12, as if ancient Republicans and Democrats each got to tell their side of the story. We meet this important feature of the Bible again and again: it is very Jewish and quite biblical to be comfortable with contrasting stories and different perspectives sitting side by side in the text. Thus we have two creation accounts (Genesis 1–2), two sets of Ten Commandments (Exodus 20; Deuteronomy 5), two narratives about the kingdoms of Israel and Judah, and so on. This trend continues in the New Testament, which has not two or three but *four* Gospel accounts, with some details that cannot be reconciled. Diversity of views seems to be part of the biblical approach.

Side note: the storytelling in First and Second Samuel is some of the very best in all the Bible, particularly concerning the tragic King Saul. Those texts are marvels of incisive character portrayal.

In any case, the kingship took hold, especially in the reign of David. David is many-faceted, a blockbuster biblical figure and the greatest king Israel ever had. He was a military mastermind and political genius; he joined the tribes in a national unity that endured for two generations; he wisely chose the capital city, Jerusalem, on the north-south border so that all might claim it. But above all, he was a heartfelt and passionate worshiper of the Lord; even God is a fan of David, the only character that the Bible calls "a man after [God's] own heart" (1 Samuel 13:14). The confirmation of this occurs in a very important passage in 2 Samuel 7. When David proposed to build God a "house," that is, a temple, God demurred; but with a clever verbal pun, God strikingly promised to build David's "house," that is, a dynasty.

David is a blockbuster biblical figure.

> I will raise up your offspring after you, sprung from your loins, and I will establish his kingdom. He it is who shall build a house [temple] for my name, and I will establish his royal throne forever. I will be a father to him, and he shall be a son to me. . . . I will not withdraw my favor from him as I withdrew it from Saul who was before you. Your house [dynasty] and your kingdom are firm forever before me; your throne shall be firmly established forever. (2 Samuel 7:12–16)

This, in effect, adds a new promise to the covenant first given to Abraham; it came from the same gracious, unobligated favor that God had shown to Abraham. Leave it to David to get a special provision for his family written into the covenant with Abraham!

David, of course, has weaknesses. He was vengeful to his enemies, and the ugly affair with Bathsheba included not just adultery, but also deceit and murder (2 Samuel 11–12). Nevertheless, the dynasty continued under Solomon, who presided over Israel's golden age of international power, wealth, and learning. Over the next four hundred years, the monarchy of the house of David endured despite the kingdom's split into two states, Israel in the north and Judah in the south. Very few of the Davidic kings of Judah were exemplary. But the mythology surrounding David's kingship created an ideology that interlocked David's political and spiritual fortunes: his dynasty was never-ending, Jerusalem was impregnable, and the Temple was indestructible. This ideology was dramatically confirmed by Jerusalem's virtually miraculous escape from invading Assyrian forces about the year 701 BC (see 2 Kings 19).

The reason is that the promise of 2 Samuel 7 was actually not just a personal favor to David. God was making a provision through David for something much greater than even he could understand and prophecy could only hint at. Its implications stretched far into the future for the New Testament and beyond, as we will see. For David's kingship became the pattern or template for a future greater son of David who would usher in a global age of peace and harmony. Isaiah, court prophet to the house of David in the eighth century BC, relates his breathtaking vision of the magnificent rule of this charismatic and powerful king of Israel:

> His dominion is vast
>   and forever peaceful,
> Upon David's throne, and over his kingdom,
>   which he confirms and sustains
> By judgment and justice,
>   both now and forever. . . .
> They shall not harm or destroy on all my holy mountain;
>   for the earth shall be filled with knowledge of the LORD,
>   as waters cover the sea.

(Isaiah 9:6, 11:9)

Isaiah thought his prophecy would be fulfilled within the history of David's political dynasty. For him the unconditional promise to David assured it. In reality, the political line was unfortunately broken with the early sixth-century invasion of the Babylonians; they disrupted the line of David, destroyed the Temple, and razed Jerusalem to the ground.

But even that disaster did not actually disconfirm the promise to David, however; on the spiritual, poetic, and mythological level, the kingship of David endured, the Temple of the LORD remained, and the holy city of Jerusalem persisted—as objects of promise and hope. The promise to David undergoes a transformation with several features. First, "the steadfast loyalty promised to David" is distributed to the whole nation ravaged by the exile (Isaiah 55:3). Second, the appearance of the kingship blessed by God is indefinitely deferred to a future date of God's own choosing. David's son is still to appear, but we do not know how or when or in what form. Third, the breadth of the kingdom widens from national Israel to peoples of the world, of all lands and races; it is now a kingdom with a cosmic scope. Fourth, and most importantly, the kingly figure himself changes; his origins are relocated from earthly Jerusalem to a throne in the heavens as Isaiah's royal "Son of David" mutates into Daniel's royal "Son of Man." In the presence of "thousands upon thousands . . . and myriads upon myriads" in God's heavenly court, the royal title is conferred upon the Son of Man, not from a dynasty but from the hand of God himself, "the Ancient of Days" (Daniel 7:9–13).

> He received dominion, splendor, and kingship;
>> all nations, peoples and tongues will serve him.
> His dominion is an everlasting dominion
>> that shall not pass away,
>> his kingship, one that shall not be destroyed.
>
> (Daniel 7:14)

By the time we come to the New Testament, the idea of kingship undergoes other transformations as well, as we will see. For now it is sufficient to say that our Lord Jesus Christ, Son of David, Son of Man, and Son of God, combines all these royal images in himself.

CHAPTER 10

Prophecy: Returning to God and Looking for Good

Read: 1 Kings 18–19; Hosea 1–2; Amos 5; Isaiah 6; Jeremiah 7.

A biblical prophet is one called to discern God's will, and to announce God's Word of judgment and salvation in a particular historical situation. The work of Israel's prophets cannot be understood apart from the covenant made with Israel at Mt. Sinai, with the Ten Commandments as its cornerstone.

The prophet was a common figure in many ancient Near Eastern cultures, not only Israel. Prophecy seems to have put people in a trance-like state that gave a special connection to the divine and made their words oracles of divine truth. We hear of prophets in the wilderness with Moses (Numbers 11:29), and a later connection between prophecy and the Sinai covenant emerges in stories about two ninth century BC prophets to the northern kingdom of Israel, Elijah and Elisha (1–2 Kings). The sequence of stories from 1 Kings 17 to 2 Kings 13 about these two powerful characters creates a gripping narrative that combines their stouthearted defense of the covenant, their prickly antagonism of corrupt kings, and their knack for working miracles.

Elijah's take-no-prisoners approach on behalf of the covenant leaves a deep impression. Because of his vigorous opposition to idolators, particularly in a confrontation on Mt. Carmel (the story told in 1 Kings 18), Elijah became a hunted man and went into hiding. He also suffered from a sort of depression, lamenting to God, "I have been most zealous for the LORD, the God of hosts, but the Israelites have forsaken your covenant. They have destroyed your altars and murdered your prophets by the sword. I alone remain, and they seek to take my life" (1 Kings 19:10). At that point he experiences the Lord in a new way, not in climactic public scenes but in quiet stillness. When God tells Elijah to "stand on the mountain"—the same one where Moses met God—the Lord passes by. Elijah witnesses "a strong and violent wind rending the mountains and crushing rocks before the LORD—but the LORD was not in the wind; after the wind an earthquake—but the LORD was not in the earthquake; after the earthquake, fire—but the LORD was not in the fire; after the fire, a light silent sound" (1 Kings 19:11–12). This paradoxical "silent sound" signaled a change in the future of prophecy. Later prophets contended for the covenant just as strenuously and passionately as the earlier Elijah, but they received the Word of the Lord like the later Elijah, in the stillness of spirit.

Whereas stories were written *about* Elijah and Elisha and their message, in the eighth century and later the very prophecies of the prophets get published. The work of "the writing prophets" began as oral proclamation artfully constructed as poetry; it was their rhythmic street preaching, so to say, recited live, that got written down by their followers. Sometimes narrators mixed in stories about the prophets whose words they relayed verbatim. Most of the prophetic books of the Bible convey actual words from Amos, Hosea, Isaiah, Jeremiah, and others. They are large in size and in importance.

What was the message of the prophets? They promoted renewed loyalty to the Sinai covenant by calling people to "return" to God (Hebrew, *shuv*); this is the root idea of

Prophets called people to a radical change of mind.

"repentance," which refers to making an about-face in one's attitude and life. Many prophetic themes flowed from this call to a radical change of mind to fully embrace the covenant. Among them are:

- condemnation of rampant idolatry and the call to worship the Lord alone;

- severe criticism of social injustices toward one's neighbors (fellow Israelites), in the call to help the poor, the widow, and the orphan;

- repudiation of hypocrisy in worship;

- promotion of authentic devotion according to the true knowledge of God—defining "knowledge" not as theory but as experience gained from steadfast, loving obedience;

- reproach of Israel for forgetting its long history and remembrance of God's constant favor to the ancestors; and

- rejection of small-minded and self-absorbed thinking that restricts God's mercy to *us* and reserves judgment for *everyone else.*

All this led to lots of stormy preaching; however, the message of judgment never appears alone or for its own sake; it always tries to bring people's hearts back to God so that he may save them. Even the severest of the prophets somewhere let the brilliant sunrays of salvation's promises burst through.

CHAPTER 11

Apocalyptic Literature:
The Sky Rains Salvation

Read: Ezekiel 37, Daniel 7, 12.

While not narrative literature in the proper sense, the apocalyptic writings presuppose the stories of the post-Exilic period (sixth century BC and later). Many stories might be mentioned here. Ezra and Nehemiah in particular tell of the rebuilding of the city of Jerusalem and the Temple, of the reinstatement of the Law to the people and the many difficulties faced. But we will focus briefly on apocalyptic literature as a way of seeing the imagined story line of the oppressed people of this time.

The main body of prophetic literature had been concerned to discern and deliver the Word of the Lord in times of need. But the unprecedented crisis of the Babylonian exile shifted this perspective, and the call to hope and perseverance became urgent. People had been car-ried off to Babylon, Jerusalem had been destroyed, the Temple burned down, and the king dethroned. The

The exiled people thought that God had disowned them.

people thought the ancient covenant had been canceled, that God had disowned them. They said, "Our hope is lost, and we are cut off" (Ezekiel 37:11). Into this dire situation came Ezekiel. The double-edged quality of his visions will later flower into the genre of apocalyptic: its frightening imagery both induces fear and at the same time produces hope. This was the effect of Ezekiel's famous vision of the valley of dry bones. Amidst a horrific picture of mass death, God commanded the prophet to speak to the bleached human bones scattered about the valley.

> Thus says the Lord GOD to these bones: Listen! I will make breath enter you so you may come to life. I will put sinews on you, make flesh grow over you, cover you with skin, and put breath into you so you may come to life. Then you shall know that I am the LORD. . . . I am going to open your graves; I will make you come up out of your graves, my people, and bring you back to the land of Israel. (Ezekiel 37:5–6, 12)

This was not about resurrection at the end of time, but a restoration of the nation in the return from the exile. When it occurred, it was a wondrous event; but rebuilding the city and Temple along with the people's faith and practice was a long and challenging task. Yet even when discouragement was constant, prophetic visions of the glorious future buoyed the people's spirits. Another prophet after the exile ended wrote: "Arise! Shine, for your light has come, / the glory of the LORD has dawned upon you. / Though darkness covers the earth, / and thick clouds, the peoples, / Upon you the LORD will dawn, / and over you his glory will be seen. / Nations shall walk by your light, / kings by the radiance of your dawning" (Isaiah 60:1–3).

However, things would get a lot worse before they got better. After a period of freedom, oppression perpetrated by the remnants of the Greek empire even led to a desecration of the Temple. These situations of threat and persecution gave rise to a distinctive genre of literature known as apocalyptic. "Apocalypse" comes from a Greek word that means "uncovering." This literature unveils secrets of God's mysterious design for history. Through a coded language of wild imagery, secret revelations are given to famous characters that explain the mysterious plan visible only in the mind of God, the Lord of history. Apocalyptic visions pull back the veil on the workings of heaven, especially in times of oppression,

"Apocalypse" comes from a Greek word that means "uncovering."

in order to instill hope. The imagery of these events cannot be taken literally; we should understand its intention to help people imagine the unimaginable, as when trying to picture peace in a time of war, or health in a time of sickness.

The central apocalyptic text of the Old Testament appears in the Book of Daniel—an enormously influential text that became a seedbed for an entire crop of apocalyptic writing that followed. Daniel's apocalyptic visions also strongly influenced the teaching of Jesus (Mark 13, Matthew 24) and other parts of the New Testament, especially the Book of Revelation. It was written in the mid-second century BC during persecution by the Seleucid ruler Antiochus IV (Epiphanes). He demanded worship of pagan gods and forbade Jewish practices, and so made himself the prototype for the classic end-time figure known as the Antichrist. This book uses the figure of a legendary prophet named Daniel and the setting of the Babylonian exile to encode a message of resolute hope in God's future victory. It envisions the empires of preceding centuries as monsters rising up from the sea of history. As threatening as these monsters seem, "the Ancient of Days," the great high God, retains his constant supremacy in hidden majesty. But then suddenly he appears in dazzling technicolor with an awesome throng of his saints.

> . . . the Ancient of Days took his throne.
> His clothing was white as snow,
>   the hair on his head like pure wool;
> His throne was flames of fire,
>   with wheels of burning fire.
> A river of fire surged forth,
>   flowing from where he sat;
> Thousands upon thousands were ministering to him,
>   and myriads upon myriads stood before him.
>
> (Daniel 7:9–1c

God is not shaken or even fazed by the horrifying creatur Daniel envisions God executing judgment upon the one evil b that controls them all. "The court was convened, and the books opened, . . . the beast was slain and its body destroyed and thrown into the burning fire" (7:10–11). Then from the sidelines appears God's own warrior. Daniel's vision of "One like a son of man" (7:13) would have tremendous impact in the future, not least upon Jesus and the early Christians. He wrote:

> As the visions during the night continued, I saw coming with the clouds of heaven
>> One like a son of man.
> When he reached the Ancient of Days
>> and was presented before him,
> He received dominion, splendor, and kingship;
>> all nations, peoples and tongues will serve him.
> His dominion is an everlasting dominion
>> that shall not pass away,
>> his kingship, one that shall not be destroyed.
>>> (Daniel 7:13–14)

This glistening future would unveil many secrets not known before this time. Most prominent among these is the disclosure of a future resurrection from the dead. Absent from virtually the whole Old Testament except for a few vague hints, this idea finally makes its bold appearance.

> Many of those who sleep
>> in the dust of the earth shall awake,
> Some to everlasting life,
>> others to reproach and everlasting disgrace.
> But those with insight shall shine brightly
>> like the splendor of the firmament,
> And those who lead the many to justice
>> shall be like the stars forever.
>>> (Daniel 12:2–3)

It must be observed that despite their intention and potential to ʳe hope and comfort, these prophetic and apocalyptic visions have ᵉrated enormous confusion and fear throughout history. People ·ifying themselves as instruments of God's righteous anger have used the militaristic imagery of these texts to fancy themselves as executors of God's justice. To this day, untutored reading by self-styled prophets stokes the magical thinking of naive readers, which has given rise, to speak frankly, to a lot of misguided hooey. Well-meaning but woodenly literal-minded believers have been taught to read the texts as if they were tabloids predicting tomorrow's headlines. All of this can be safely ignored.

But how should we read these texts? The best help is to try to understand the intentions of their authors, and to discern the historical context in which they worked. A state of emergency moved apocalyptic writers to create an entirely new strain of prophetic literature. Desperate times called for desperate measures: they designed this extreme visionary literature to subvert the oppressor's power and electrify the people's hope. Above all, we should keep in mind that the ultimate intention of all apocalyptic writers and their texts was to inspire hope.

CHAPTER 12

The Gospel of the Lord

Read: Mark 8:27–30.

The Gospel, with its four accounts, stands at the center of the Christian Bible, a brilliant beacon sweeping its light across all the rest of the Scriptures and pointing the way for reading them well. Its events, people, deeds, and words converge upon salvation's fulfillment, a fourfold story set within the frame of a single great climactic event that achieves it: the Death of Jesus, King of the Jews, whom God made Lord and Christ. Just as the Beloved Disciple of the Gospel according to John saw blood and water gush from our Lord's side after he died (John 19:34), so in hearing the Gospel we become witnesses of Christ's saving love pouring out upon the world from his heart. All of this is embodied and implied in the honors that we bestow upon the *Book of the Gospels* at Mass.

Earlier, in Part 1, we identified hearing Scripture as an "audible sacrament," one of the characteristics of a Catholic way of reading Scripture. The Second Vatican Council taught Catholics that Scripture and Sacrament have one source: The Church . . . unceasingly receives and offers to the faithful the bread of life from the table both of God's word and of Christ's body.[1]

The *Book of the Gospels* upon the altar during the Liturgy of the Word is an icon of this. Likewise our reading of the Gospel has a direct relationship to our reception of the Eucharist. As Christ nourishes us by his Body and Blood under the appearances of bread and wine, so Christ comes to us in the proclaimed Word. The Council

---

DV, 21

Fathers likewise stressed this: "Christ is present in his word, since it is he himself who speaks when the holy Scriptures are read in the Church."[2] The Gospel, then, is a sort of Eucharist in words. It reminds us that when we receive the Lord's Body and Blood, we receive not only the Lord in his mysterious divine presence; we receive the Lord bundled together within all his turbulent human history intact as told in the Gospel accounts. In receiving the sacrament we take up the Lord's human reality in all its aspects: his human conception in the womb of his Jewish mother, all the storms and stresses of growing up, and all the interactions described in the stories we read about when he talked and enacted God's Kingdom, leading to his sacred Death, Resurrection, and Ascension into heaven, where his holy humanity awaits our communion with him and each other forever.

It is every Christian's duty and delight to read, ponder, savor, and pray the Gospels. In truth there is one Gospel, presented to us in four accounts. Not everything in them is equally clear, and much about their making is unknown. We don't really know who wrote them; none is signed, and the names we attach to them come from second century Church tradition. But such obscurities don't block us from reading and trusting—and enjoying—these marvelous books. The stories about our Lord make vivid his beautiful human character and the diamond-hard reality of his divine identity. The narratives are clear, the teaching is deep, and the inspiration is strong. When you first read these accounts, you'll find lots of gold nuggets of wisdom and spiritual teaching lying everywhere, free for the taking. This is especially true of these Gospel stories, where something valuable for everyone appears on every page, no matter how often we've read them.

---

2. SC, 7.

Beginning to Read the Gospel Accounts—Appreciating the Differences

In ages past, the Church was preoccupied with a single clear message about Jesus coming from the four Gospel accounts, and saw little difference among them. The differences were harmonized so they could be read interchangeably. But modern study has helped us to understand that the differences among the accounts are unavoidable and significant. We've also realized that, in the light of faith, these differences are not contradictions that threaten faith, but variations that enrich it. We learn from their subtly different ways of teaching about our Lord that going from one to another is like making a transition from two-dimensional to three-dimensional imagery; instead of expecting the flat clarity and precision of a photograph, we should read as though taking in a sculpture by circling it from different angles.

The Gospel accounts do not merely rehearse facts; they explore deeds and words for their symbolic power and importance for faith. Each Gospel account does this in a different way, but John's account encapsulates the approach by selecting events in our Lord's ministry to ponder as "signs"—the Gospel's own word for them—that capture and lovingly contemplate his glory. This contemplative way of reading Scripture parallels the Church's characteristically Catholic way of devotedly meditating on every aspect of Christ as a way of deepening faith—a practice noted by Bl. John Henry Newman:

> The energetic, direct apprehension of an unseen Lord and Saviour has not been peculiar to Prophets and Apostles; it has been the habit of His Holy Church and of her children, down to this day. Age passes after age, and she varies her discipline, and she adds to her devotions, and all with the one purpose of fixing her own and their gaze more fully upon the person of her unseen Lord. She has adoringly surveyed him, feature by feature, and has paid a separate homage to him in every one. She has made us honour His Five Wounds, His Precious Blood, and His Sacred Heart. She has bid us meditate upon His infancy, and the acts of His ministry; His agony, His scourging, and His crucifixion. She has sent

us on a pilgrimage to His birthplace and His sepulchre, and the mountain of His ascension. She has sought out and placed before us, the memorials of His life and death; His crib and holy house, His holy tunic, the handkerchief of St Veronica, the cross and its nails, His winding-sheet, and the napkin for His head. (Newman, *Occasional Sermons*).

This urge for loving contemplation of our Lord has in all ages given fresh access to his sacred humanity. The Catholic way of reading Scripture—including the Gospel texts—does the same thing.

The reconstituted *Lectionary*, designed after the Second Vatican Council, seized the teaching opportunity of focusing on the perspective of one Gospel each year. So we now have a three-year Lectionary cycle that reads Matthew in Year A, Mark in Year B, and Luke in Year C. John does not have its own year, for the Church puts forward John's deeply spiritual perspective every year during special seasons, especially Christmas, Holy Week, the Sacred Paschal Triduum, and Easter. Every year the readings dive deeply into each Gospel's distinctive contribution. Like turning a diamond in light, the Church meditates upon the beauty of Jesus from all the angles provided by the different viewpoints of each Gospel.

At the Center: Who Then Is Jesus?

Jesus himself puts forward this question, and it has relevance for any reader of the Gospel: "Who do you say that I am?" (Mark 8:29; Matthew 16:15; Luke 9:20). The directness of the challenge is captured in the painting of Christ's face by the fifteenth century Dutch artist, Hans Memling. With hand held up in a sign of blessing, Jesus serenely but seriously looks through the picture frame into viewer eyes. "Who do you say that I am?" Gazing upon our Lord's face a awaits our answer, we realize that his whole attention is fixed us; he is not busy feeding five thousand, or walking on a healing a paralytic, or answering the jibes of his critics. As meet his at this moment, he is concerned with you and you alone. It is an image that every Gospel reading might suggest to us.

Whether we approach the Gospel as committed believers in the house of faith or bewildered and curious outsiders, we can't escape the designs that these texts have upon us. They insist that we make a decision about Jesus Christ, for good or for ill. John's Gospel account sees this clearly, showing how Jesus' hearers couldn't decide whether to acclaim him or arrest him: "There was considerable murmuring about him in the crowds. Some said, 'He is a good man,' [while] others said, 'No, on the contrary, he misleads the crowd'" (John 7:12). The evangelist commented dryly, "So a division occurred in the

Christ Giving His Blessing, 1478, by Hans Memling, Norton Simon Museum.

crowd because of him" (7:43). Some tentatively believed Jesus to be the Messiah; they followed spontaneously and remained with him even in difficulty. As Peter said at one point, "Master, to whom shall we go? You have the words of eternal life" (John 6:68). For others Jesus was "a sign that will be contradicted," as old Simeon foretold when he held the baby at the Temple (Luke 2:34). Not a few people profoundly doubted Jesus; even some of his family thought he was "out of his mind" (Mark 3:21). Others saw him as diabolical, saying he drove out demons by the prince of demons (Mark 3:22). Herod the ᵗrarch thought he was John the Baptist raised from the dead atthew 14:2). Others thought he was Elijah returning, or a prophet ʳeremiah (Matthew 16:14). Some authorities, sent to arrest him, ed their minds and came back empty handed, explaining, ᵇefore has anyone spoken like this one" (John 7:46).

ᵖoint is this: if one is truly paying attention, there's no mid-
between being for or against Jesus. Push comes to shove

in the view that one takes of Jesus' Death and Resurrection, the event that climaxes the Gospel story and defines his identity. This was the major dividing point between stories that were accepted into the New Testament, and the many imitators

> In Christianity, the same One who first *proclaimed* the message ultimately *became* the message.

that were not. In the second century, different groups categorized as "Gnostics" failed to meet the standard of addressing Jesus' deepest identity in his Death and Resurrection. For them, Jesus was *only* the revealer of secret, hidden divine wisdom for salvation. Similarly, some modern reinterpretations of Jesus see him as *only* a revolutionary, or *only* a wisdom teacher, or *only* an apocalyptic firebrand, or *only* everybody's undemanding good friend. But this *"only* approach" inevitably reduces Jesus to a one-dimensional figure, and virtually always avoids dealing with the canonical Gospels' explosive claim about his human Death and Resurrection.

So we explore in Matthew, Mark, Luke, and John the fourfold witness that the ancient Church tested and found fruitful for entering more deeply into communion with the God-Man of the Gospel. Typically John makes explicit what is implicit in the first three "synoptic" Gospel accounts. Jesus, in John's account, does not wait for others to answer the question about who he is; rather he boldly asserts his identity: "I am the bread of life" (6:35); "I am the light of the world" (8:12); "I am the good shepherd" (10:11); "I am the resurrection and the life" (11:25). These statements reveal something essential not only about John and the other Gospel accounts, but also about Christianity itself—and this is something that makes Christian faith distinctive among the world's great religions.

Christianity shares a great many values and viewpoints with other faiths. With other faiths, Christians follow a great wisdom figure as their primary teacher who points the way to a higher life. Jesus, too, points to the Kingdom of God, just as Moses points to the way of the covenant, Mohammed points to the way of Allah, a

Buddha points to the way of enlightenment, and so on. However, in Christianity, the same One who first *proclaimed* the message ultimately *became* the message. Jesus proclaimed the Kingdom of God, but the Apostles proclaimed Jesus. Later writers like Origen analyzed that Jesus himself became the Kingdom he proclaimed. To respond to him was to respond to the Kingdom; to believe in him was to enter the Kingdom. So the person of Jesus himself is uniquely central to Christianity, and this makes Christianity different. This distinctive "Way" appears explicitly in John's Gospel account when Jesus says, "I am the way and the truth and the life" (John 14:6). Jesus himself is crucial to Christian faith, its source and center and fullness. Jesus himself brings about a new way of seeing and living that depends utterly upon him and upon the life that he brings to his followers.

CHAPTER 13

The Gospel of the Lord: Reading to Believe and Understand

Read: Luke 1:1–4; John 20:31.

> Faith inquires, ponders, and seeks to understand.

The Gospel accounts, then, are not mere descriptions or historical accounts; these narratives aim to persuade you to answer authentically Jesus' urgent question, "Who do you say that I am?" To get a sense of the attitude with which the serious seeking Catholic reads these texts, let's look briefly at the faith perspective of two great Catholic readers of Scripture, St. Augustine (fourth century) and St. Anselm (eleventh century). Augustine made the Latin version of Isaiah 7:9 a sort of motto for how to come to know God: "Unless you believe, you will not understand." Anselm honed Augustine's model with a saying that remains to this day a good thumbnail description of theology: "faith seeking understanding."

The outlook of Augustine and Anselm points out for our rational minds a way forward for questioning. Notice the travel metaphor here. When we start out, we obviously want to point ourselves in the right direction, for the first step determines all the rest. Similarly when we desire to think of God rightly, our first move is cruc— because it affects all later thinking about God. Faith is that star— point. However, the thinking process doesn't end there, for fait— pels our minds to reach forward toward what (or whom) one b— Like seeing a majestic mountain in the distance, believir— gaze and spontaneously move closer for a better view, r—

reach the mountain and climb it. Thus faith inquires, ponders, and seeks to understand, like Mary meditating continually on the events surrounding her Son, when she "kept all these things, reflecting on them in her heart" (Luke 2:19). Catholics read the Gospel accounts in a similar inquisitive and contemplative way. True faith desires to know the one it believes in, just as love longs to become complete by knowing its beloved.

This suggests a two-stage process for reading the Gospel accounts. First, we read *in order to believe in Christ*, and then while believing, we read *in order to understand Christ*. (A third stage naturally follows: we read *in order to love and obey Christ*, that is, to live a disciple's life of prayer and service. Here we're speaking only of starting that process.) Two texts from the Gospel can help to spell out these two stages. They function like bookends that set a framework for viewing the reader's progress from faith to understanding. The two texts are John 20:31 and Luke 1:1–4. Let's look at them both more closely. (In these quotations below, the italics are mine.)

"Believe": John 20:31 and Stories for Sparking Faith

> These [stories about Jesus' signs] are *written that you may [come to] believe* that Jesus is the Messiah, the Son of God, and that through this belief [that is, through the act of believing] you may have life in his name. (John 20:31; emphasis added)

The first text occurs after the story of Jesus has been told, and focuses on the evangelist's purpose for writing: to induce "believing." John has spoken of Jesus' earthly ministry in terms of a series of "signs" that revealed his divinity and portrayed his love. John says that Jesus performed many signs that couldn't be included in his ~~b~~ok. But then he writes: "These are written that you may come to ~~beli~~eve." This statement summarizes well John's reason for writing, ~~and~~ can also stand as a purpose statement for all four Gospel ~~accoun~~ts, and perhaps even for the whole New Testament. Let's ~~examine~~ its parts.

1. *"Written"*: That the story of Jesus gets written down is a basic feature of Christianity, and the written text is an effective mediator, not only of Jesus' story, but also of his real presence. We are not beneath the Apostles as Christians, despite their privileges; in order to partake fully of his grace, we do not need to have been physically present as eyewitnesses to our Lord's Death and Resurrection. Indeed he has just told once-unbelieving Thomas, "Have you come to believe because you have seen me? Blessed are those who have not seen and have believed" (John 20:29). The texts translate Jesus' life and presence into a mode that is accessible in all times and places.

2. *"That you may come to believe"*: The essential reason that the Gospel accounts were written down was to generate the response of faith. The words on the page mediate the power of God to impact human lives. Believing is the distinctive human response to what God has done, a lesson taught long before by Abraham, as we have seen (Genesis 15:6; Romans 4:3–4). This act of believing does more than accept an idea or learn new knowledge; it is an act of trust and self-investment that surrenders one's heart to another, betting all the chips of one's life, so to say, on Jesus and his teaching. The act is not self-generated; we don't drum up faith from within: it grows as a *response* to the story that is heard. Thus John's statement comes at the end of his Gospel account, after he has told the story of Jesus. Together with the Sacrament of Baptism, the act of believing is our response that begins the Christian life.

3. *"That Jesus is the Messiah, the Son of God"*: What—or rather *whom*—does one come to believe? Faith in the Christian sense is not a blind leap of trust, but a rational act of investing oneself in some- one who is very specific, with a story told by credible witnesses, a story that defines, reveals, and commends him. Believing in Jesus is just as coherent and rational as entrusting yourself to a doctor when you're sick. Jesus is more than an admirably good person, heroic in virtue, with a record of kindness; he was the long-awaited Messiah of Israel and Son of God. Three characters portrayed in the Old Testament prefigured him; they were transformative figures, char

agents who would lead Israel's transition from the present evil age into the glorious age to come. First, the royal "Son of David" appeared in Isaiah 9 and 11 as "a child is born to us" (9:5) who would "judge the poor with justice" (11:4) and an era of peace so transformative that even natural animal enemies would become friends (11:6–8). Second, the "Servant of the Lord" emerged in Isaiah 40–55; he resembles the Son of David insofar as he brings justice to the nations (42:1), but differs from him in that he does so without raising his voice or dousing a wick (42:2–3). Rather he brings justice by mysteriously suffering for others as a self-offering that resembles the sacrifices of the Temple (53:4–6). Third, the "Son of Man" in Daniel 7 is neither an earthly royal figure nor a man of suffering, but rather a divine being, an apocalyptic figure who ceremoniously receives dominion from God's own hand in the heavens (7:13–14). In the New Testament, *our Lord Jesus Christ is all three.* To entrust oneself to Jesus, therefore, is to enter into a relationship with a person of generous royalty, compassionate sympathy, and awesome power.

4. *"So that you may have life in his name":* The act of believing in this God-man, whom John pictures as a walking temple of God on earth (2:21), does something extraordinary to us. It communicates the very divine life of Jesus to his human followers. John, and Jesus in John, often refers to "life," and the word appears often in this Gospel account. The Greek word used for "life" is zōē, from which we get our word "zoo"; it appears more than twenty-five times in John. The common ancient meaning of zōē went beyond mere vegetative existence (*bios*) to speak of sentient life, or life with consciousness. John adapts zōē to speak of that mysterious wondrous reality called "eternal life."

We should note four things packed into the phrase "eternal life." First, the word "eternal" means more than just "endless." It refers to a *new kind of life;* "eternal life" literally means "life of the Age (to come)." The prophets contrast life in our present evil age with life in "the age to come" which is characterized by peace, health, and salvation. That the "life of the Age" that John refers to. So "eternal" here refers not quantity but to *quality* of life. Second, this life is nothing other than *the life of God*, who is the source of life. Whoever receives eternal life lives by the same life that characterizes God's own life, life that is indestructibly deep, unimaginably rich, and endlessly plentiful. Third, this life comes to us *through Jesus*. This has two aspects: it begins in creation and culminates in re-creation. When John writes, "What came to be through him was life" (1:3c–4), he is speaking of creation. When he writes, "Whoever believes in the Son has eternal life" (3:36), he is writing about re-creation. Similarly, the Psalms call the Father "the living God" (Psalm 42:3) who "has decreed a blessing, / life for evermore!" (Psalm 133:3). The Father's abundant life has granted the Son to have "life in himself" (John 5:26). He sent his Son to us, and instructed him about what to say, for "his commandment is eternal life" (12:50). Fourth, eternal life is not only about the future, but is a *present possession of believers*, who have been "born of God" (1:13), and have already "passed from death to life" (5:24). Jesus is constantly giving his life to believers "abundantly" (10:10). John wrote his Gospel account in order to initiate people into a life of believing in the Son of God. To read and believe is to enter into the mystery of Jesus.

"Understand": Luke 1:1–4 and Teaching for Depth of Faith

> Since many have undertaken to compile a narrative of the events that have been fulfilled among us, . . . I too have decided, after investigating everything accurately anew, to write it down in an orderly sequence for you, most excellent Theophilus, *so that you may realize the certainty of the teachings you have received.* (Luke 1:1, 3–4; emphasis added)

The second statement comes from Luke's preface to the third Gospel account, where he tells Theophilus upfront that he intends to advance believers like him to a new level of understanding. While John wrote in order to stir readers to believe, Luke wrote to sti[r] believers to study and understand what they believe. (In reality, [of] course, both Gospel accounts nourish both the beginner and [the] advanced; that is, they each promote both believing and unders[tand]ing). Luke wrote his thorough and artful review of Jesus' bir[th,] words, deeds, Death, Resurrection, and Ascension in order t[o] faith more securely. Luke's short introduction addresses a correspondent, Theophilus. Whether or not Theophilus was a real person, the name that means "friend of God" symbolizes all new believers looking for spiritual depth. Luke says that he writes as a second generation Christian, which means he did not personally meet Jesus. This alone reassures readers who come long after Jesus' time that they are not at a disadvantage. Like John, he writes with full confidence that one can just as surely know Jesus through the pages of the text as the disciples knew him face-to-face.

Luke carefully investigated the stories about Jesus that "eyewitnesses from the beginning and ministers of the word have handed down to us," and then decided to write his own "orderly sequence" as a Christian historian and teacher. Verse 4 delivers the punch line as Luke explains his purpose for writing: "so that you may realize the certainty of the teachings you have received." Each part of this verse is important, even if the vividness in Luke's language gets lost in our translation. The Greek word here as "realize" means "to know thoroughly, exactly, to grasp through and through." Luke intends to give us advanced training in the traditions about Jesus. The word translated "certainty" suggests a quite concrete image rather than an abstract attitude; it envisions walking along a path without stumbling, that is, being "sure footed." This suggests two ideas: the truths themselves are secure, and also one may grasp them with full assurance. The "teachings that you have received" literally means, "the words that you were taught." "Words" surely refers to more than individual words, for it can mean concepts, or stories, or subjects, and other ideas. The word for "taught" literally means, "to echo sounds down to someone." The echo concept is embedded in our ʾords for handing on Christian teaching, "catechesis" and "cateʾsm." Christians "echo" the truth about Jesus in the stable pattern ʾaching about him that is handed on from generation to genera-ʾlthough Christian teaching grows and blossoms over time, its ʾy truths are firmly rooted and grounded.

CHAPTER 14

The Gospel of the Lord: The Genius of Four-Way Viewing

Read: Matthew 27; Mark 15; Luke 23; John 19.

What does having a fourfold Gospel mean for serious readers of the Bible? It's important to acknowledge that Scripture offers differing portraits of the Lord; but if we understand how symbolism works, we can see that the four versions are supplementary, not contradictory.

Mark, for instance, emphasizes *Jesus the suffering Son of Man*, who "did not come to be served but to serve and to give his life as a ransom for many" (Mark 10:45). Matthew does not disagree with or negate the image of the suffering Son of Man, but includes it in his narrative while emphasizing a different picture, *Jesus the teaching Messiah*. Although Jesus certainly teaches in the other Gospel accounts, Matthew uniquely features page after page of Jesus just talking, in at least five lengthy discourses. Only in Matthew do we find Jesus saying multiple times in reference to the teaching of the Law, "You have heard that it was said . . . but I say to you" (Matthew 5:21–48). Luke, for his part, includes the suffering Son of Man and the teaching Messiah, but also loves to lift up stories about *Jesus the healing Savior*. In an important statement, Jesus summarizes his mission: "The Son of Man has come *to seek and to save* what was lost" (Luke 19:10; emphasis added). That image is not absent in the other Gospels, but Luke stresses the link that is embedded in the Greek word *sōzō*, which means at the same time both "to heal" and "to save." So after he forgives a woman in the house of Simon the Pharisee, his f word to her in some translations reads, "Your faith has saved you," while others have, "Your faith has healed you" (Luke 7:50). Both are correct. Luke uses the word for both physical and spiritual healings.

John has a special mission to emphasize Jesus as a divine messenger who reveals the Father to the world, not only by *what he says and does* but also even more by *who he is*. John adapts the ancient image of Dame Wisdom from Proverbs and Sirach to portray *Jesus the Wisdom of God in flesh*. He not only speaks the Word of God; he *is* the Word of God come into the world (John 1:14). In John, so closely does Jesus identify with God that he can say, "The Father and I are one" (10:30), and "Whoever has seen me has seen the Father" (14:9).

The Synoptic Vision: The Gospel in Triplicate

Mark is the shortest of the four Gospel accounts, and the best place to enter into reading them. In doing so, readers trace the development of the Gospel tradition itself, which most scholars believe began with Mark about the year 70. He invented, so to speak, the form of a Gospel account as a new way of preaching Christ; something new was called for, perhaps in the wake of the deaths of Peter and Paul and the recent earth-shaking events in Judea during Rome's war with the Jews.

As we can see from Peter's speeches in the Acts of the Apostles or from Paul's letters, the heart of the Apostles' preaching was the Death, Resurrection, Ascension, and Second Coming of Jesus. But stories about Jesus' earthly life and ministry also circulated among believers. Mark seems to have been the one to combine the two, that is, to arrange the stories of Jesus' ministry and the account of his Death and Resurrection into a single coherent narrative.

So successful was Mark's project that other powerful theologian-storytellers took it up and expanded the tradition in later decades. Matthew and Luke probably had Mark in front of them as they wrote; their accounts in some ways are like revised and expanded editions of Mark. Comparisons of chapters and verses can be imprecise (they were inserted centuries later), but they can give a rough sketch of real differences between the four accounts. Mark's sixteen chapters contrast with Matthew's twenty-eight and Luke's twenty-four. Of just over 650 verses in Mark, Matthew includes more than six hundred of them, or more than ninety percent. Luke uses fewer, but still plenty, about fifty percent. Only three percent of Mark's verses (fewer than twenty-five) appear in John.

Matthew and Luke each reproduced and reshaped Mark, and then added new stories and sayings from several other sources. This is an impressive example of the communal development of the Jesus tradition within early Christianity. Matthew and Luke share a source (scholars call this hypothetical document "Q" from the German word for "source," *quelle*) that contains stories and sayings like the healing of the centurion's servant (Matthew 8:5–13; Luke 7:1–10) and the Lord's Prayer (Matthew 6:9–13; Luke 11:1–4).

But Matthew and Luke each used special sources with stories and sayings of Jesus found nowhere else. Matthew's stories about Jesus' infancy focused on Joseph and foreshadowed the Lord's suffering (chapters 1–2); he also conveyed special narratives featuring Peter walking upon the water (14:28–31) or retrieving the Temple tax from the mouth of a fish (17:24–27). Matthew quoted sayings of Jesus found nowhere else, such as his Wisdom-inspired invitation, "Come to me, all you who labor and are burdened, and I will give you rest" (11:28–30). He included parables like the Workers in the Vineyard (20:1–16); he reported certain legends like Judas hanging himself (27:3–10) and the resurrected saints walking about Jerusalem after the Lord's Death (27:52–53).

For his part, Luke drew on special stories about Jesus' infancy of Jesus that focus on Mary and exult in the glory of the Lord's appearing (chapters 1–2). He conveyed narratives like Jesus conversing in the Temple as a twelve-year-old (2:41–52), visiting his friends Mary and Martha (10:38–42), healing the ear of the high priest's servant trying to arrest him (22:51), and discussing Scripture with two disciples on the road to Emmaus on the day of his Resurrection (24:13–35). He quoted sayings of Jesus found nowhere else, like encouragement to the thief on the cross, "Today you will be with me in Paradise" (23:43), and memorable parables like the Good Samaritan (10:29–37), the Lost Son (15:11–32), the Rich Man and Lazarus (16:19–31) and the Pharisee and the Tax Collector (18:9–14).

Four Accounts for Four Audiences

A simple exercise can show how the four Gospel accounts work together with their distinctive differences. A comparative reading of the four accounts of the Lord's Crucifixion (Matthew 27; Mark 15; Luke 23; John 19) shows much that is similar: the presence of soldiers, the crowds, the mocking from various quarters, last words of Jesus heard and recorded, the presence of women disciples.

But notice the subtle differences among them also. The wording on the placard above Jesus' head—the only clear record we have of something written about Jesus during his lifetime—is slightly different in each Gospel account. Moreover, after Jesus dies, the statement of the centurion standing guard in Matthew and Mark ("Truly this man was the Son of God"; Mark 15:39; Matthew 27:54—nearly identical) is noticeably different from that of Luke: "This man was innocent beyond doubt" (Luke 23:47). Furthermore, Jesus in Mark and Matthew utters last words that come from one of the great biblical laments, Psalm 22: "My God, my God, why have you forsaken me?" (Mark 15:34, Matthew 27:46: Psalm 22:2). These words speak of agony and suffering, but are also a prayer of hope. Luke shifts focus to an equally compelling but quite different prayer of trust, Psalm 31: "Father, into your hands I commend my spirit" (Luke 23:46; Psalm 31:6). The words speak of complete and serene surrender, being a prayer of peace and sorrowful acceptance. In John's account, Jesus speaks not a prayer but an acclamation (John 19:30): "It is finished!" This is not a cry of despair, surprise, or even trust, but rather a shout ⁀triumph and joy. Jesus is like an artist putting the last stroke on a ⸀sterpiece. In the end, even after combining the similar pictures in

Mark and Matthew, we are left with three very different portrayals of Jesus' final moments.

> Each evangelist tied his account to the needs of his audience.

What should we make of this? It is neither satisfying nor sufficient simply to say that all these things happened. That leaves unanswered the question *why* each evangelist chose that particular final saying to portray the Lord's Death, and what, if anything, that means for understanding each Gospel account. Fr. Raymond Brown, who wrote meticulous and big scholarly books, also condensed them in short books that simplified his insights. One small jewel is his book *A Crucified Christ in Holy Week*, which brilliantly shows how each account of the Passion was not written abstractly as a mere chronicle of events. Rather each evangelist tied his account deeply to the needs of the audience for whom he was writing. Every Christian looks to the Lord for instruction, comfort, and encouragement in the task of becoming a disciple, and the texts reflect that. We can, therefore, draw a portrait of the first readers who are reflected , as in a mirror, in each Gospel account's portrait of Jesus.

For Fr. Brown, the different forms of the Lord's last words reflect different needs among Christians in the process of dying. First, for those who die in desperation and anxiety, these words of Jesus become their own: "My God, my God, why have you forsaken me?" (Matthew 27:46; Mark 15:34). For them, *Jesus is present as they face death with a questioning heart.* Second, for those who die in some sadness but also in resignation and trust, these words of Jesus become their own: "Into your hands I commend my spirit" (Luke 23:46). For them, *Jesus is present as they face death with a surrendering heart.* Third, for those who die at the end of the great struggle, exhausted but victorious, these words of Jesus become their own: "It is finished!" (John 19:30). For them, *Jesus is present as they face death with an exultant hear* All three versions of Jesus' final moment, while respecting the ba story of the tradition, served different needs within the commu This typifies how the common Gospel tradition produced accounts that stretched out in different directions to meet the needs of varying audiences.

A Way to Approach the Fourfold Gospel

This book's approach to reading the Gospel is to begin with Mark, the shortest and the fastest-paced of the four Gospel accounts, and an excellent base from which to branch out to the other synoptic accounts, Matthew and Luke. By doing this, we are retracing the historical steps of the accounts themselves, since Mark was the first written account that Matthew and Luke expanded upon.

The payoff for this approach is that once you've worked through Mark and grasped its basics, you've already learned much of Matthew and Luke (and some of John). Mark gives a solid introduction to the Jesus tradition by showing the basic "way of seeing" him. After treating Mark, we'll return to the distinctive themes in Matthew's Gospel account. Then we'll pay special attention to the magnificent and irreplaceable Christmas narratives about Jesus' conception and birth, first in Matthew, then in Luke. That will be the doorway to work with the special themes in Luke's Gospel. It's helpful to work with Luke last because unlike the other Gospel accounts, it has a sequel, the Acts of the Apostles, which tells the story of Christianity's spread in the generation after Jesus. Luke undoubtedly wanted his two books to be read together, and wouldn't be happy that the canon has split them up. Moreover, because the early Christian community's story in the last half of Acts focuses upon Paul, that leaves a natural opening to consider the letters of the New Testament, though we don't undertake that here.

CHAPTER 15

The Gospel According to Mark: Not to Be Served but to Serve

Read: entire Gospel according to Mark.

One should read Mark not as a mere chronicle but as a deeply religious presentation that is more like a portrait than a photograph, more like a dramatic film than a documentary. Like the other Gospel accounts, Mark presents Christ in order to lead readers to faith, but then goes on to deepen their understanding of him. Its rough-cut style and breathless pace may lead one to think it was hurriedly put together. But the style is part of the strategy. Mark gives us one of the most skillfully told stories in the Bible. It creatively blends paradox, irony, and misunderstanding with an alluring vision of the majestic Kingdom of God that is about to break in upon us. The central character is Jesus, of course, but his portrait is complex. He's both deeply human and awesomely divine, a preacher of God's Kingdom who lavishly pours compassion on everyone, but also a demanding teacher who leaves his disciples panting to keep up. Most surprising to everyone in the story, he becomes "a man of suffering" (Isaiah 53:3), who "did not come to be served but to serve and to give his life as a ransom for many" (Mark 10:45, a key summary statement). Suffering and abandonment reveal the deepest layers of his identity (Mark 15:39). Furthermore, against all expectation, Mark portrays Jesus' disciples in a way that is, so to say, unsuitable for holy cards. After starting well they fall short in almost every thought and deed. However, we find that Mark has adopted a strategy here, for he uses them to teach his readers to learn from the first followers failures. Meanwhile, he offers arresting miniportraits of true discipleship through a series of minor characters that pass on and off the stage of his drama.

A few distinct themes dominate Mark's presentation; serious readers can take advantage of their clarity to grasp the Gospel quickly: Jesus' ministry for the Kingdom of God, Mark's portrayal of the unveiling of Christ's identity, and Mark's portrait of discipleship.

Jesus Proclaims the Kingdom of God: This Is the Time of Fulfillment

The crucial text here is Mark 1:15. After John the Baptist was arrested, Jesus began to preach, "This is the time of fulfillment. The kingdom of God is at hand. Repent, and believe in the Gospel." Each part of this verse is important.

1. *"This is the time of fulfillment"*: Fulfillment is a key idea in the New Testament, and this word turns up constantly. It recalls promises made in the time of the prophets concerning the age to come. The Bible has a strong sense about the right moment for the right thing to take place, of the ripeness of time. Paul wrote that God sent his Son "when the fullness of time had come" (Galatians 4:4), and that Christ died for us "at the appointed time" (Romans 5:6). Jesus announces that time's fruit is now ripe for God's ancient promises to be fulfilled.

2. *"The kingdom of God is at hand"*: Jesus here introduces the central image of his preaching. While God was always King, he is now about to exert that kingship in a new way by taking back territory stolen and perverted by the unholy robber-kingdom of evil. So this is the declaration of an impending heavenly invasion. Jesus' language of the Kingdom being "at hand" is artfully ambiguous. In Jesus the powers of the Kingdom are fully present; still he does not yet perform the world transformation that the prophets expected (Isaiah :6–10). For now is not the time for judgment, but for repentance.

3. *"Repent"*: People make themselves ready for the invasion by choosing to side with God, the heavenly invader, by putting away evil deeds and turning hearts toward him. The call to repent drives down into our inner attitudes and choices. It relates back to the call of Israel's ancient prophets to return to the covenant. It refers not to minor midcourse corrections, but to an about-face, a 180-degree turn, changing from seeing things as we're accustomed to seeing them to the way God sees them (see Mark 8:33, where Peter learns this lesson the hard way). Repentance begins by seeing things from God's perspective.

4. *"Believe in the Gospel"*: But the change is not simply about avoiding something bad; it is about embracing something good. The word "gospel" translates a Greek word that means "(sensational) good news." Jesus comes to announce God's forgiveness, healing, and harmony, a new divine-human order whose amnesty brings back even abject sinners and abhorrent outcasts.

What Is the Kingdom?

Jesus never defines the Kingdom in textbook fashion, and neither does Mark. It rather emerges in actions and stories. Looked at that way, *at least eight aspects of the Kingdom begin to appear.* Let's start with Mark 1:21–28. Jesus teaches in the synagogue and astonishes people by his teaching "for he taught them as one having authority and not as the scribes" (1:22). But Mark never tells us what he said! Jesus' deed is his Word about the Kingdom: we come to understand the Kingdom more by what Jesus does than by what he says. From the string of stories Mark narrates, we can see that "Kingdom" refers to God's action rather than to a place. And so here's the first aspect we come to understand about that action: *the Kingdom conquers evil.*

In the same chapter Jesus heals a man afflicted by a skin disease, a "leper," who was an outcast by ancient religious and social standards that tried to protect the healthy in the community against social and religious contamination. (Think of the isolation caused

Ebola during the 2014–15 African outbreak.) Jesus touches the man in order to heal him, but also sends him to the religious authorities to certify the healing and his restoration to the community. Jesus was concerned to relieve not only outer, but also inner suffering. This too was the Kingdom in action: *the Kingdom restores outcasts.*

In the healing story that begins the next chapter (Mark 2:1–12), Jesus is teaching in his house in Capernaum when a paralytic is lowered through the roof by friends to obtain the man's healing. "When Jesus saw their faith, he said to the paralytic, 'Child, your sins are forgiven'" (Mark 2:5). When this antagonizes the religious leaders, Jesus makes a point of connecting forgiveness to the man's healing, which he then completes. The metaphor is clear and potent: the Kingdom does more than heal bodies; it reaches down into each person's deepest sickness: *the Kingdom heals hearts.*

A little further on, Jesus feasts at the house of Levi with many other tax collectors and sinners—over the objections of the religious leaders. Jesus sees table fellowship as an essential part of his mission. "Those who are well do not need a physician," he says, "but the sick do. I have not come to call the righteous but sinners" (Mark 2:17). Further on, when Jesus points to the motley crew around him, he declares, "Here are my mother and my brothers. [For] whoever does the will of God is my brother and sister and mother" (Mark 3:34–35). Jesus' actions constitute a new family around him: *the Kingdom creates a new community.*

Later Jesus tells a parable (4:26–29; only in Mark) about a man who scatters seed on the land, and sleeps and wakes each day while the seed sprouts and grows. The man himself does nothing to cause the growth, and does not know how growth happens; but he gratefully reaps the harvest. Jesus says, "This is how it is with the kingdom of God" (4:26). People cooperate with the Kingdom's arrival and growth, but cannot cause or control it: *the Kingdom grows of itself by God's gift.*

Jesus tells the so-called Parable of the Sower that actually es on the types of soil, looking for the rich and productive type that will give the greatest yield. Throughout the Gospel Jesus looks for the fertile hearts to receive his words. How does one become receptive to the Kingdom of God and produce a yield? A lesson later in this chapter gives a clue and warning. When Jesus crosses the lake with his disciples and is roused from sleep by terrified disciples to quiet a threatening storm, he asks pointedly, "Do you not yet have faith?" (Mark 4:40): *the Kingdom demands faith.*

In a later episode, Jesus encountered a man with many possessions who wished to know what one must do to inherit eternal life (Mark 10:17–31). Although the man had kept all the commandments, he was clearly missing something big about the Kingdom. The spiritual physician then reaches into the man's heart, probing for spiritual blockages, feeling for what was hardening his heart. When he finds the problem and tells the man to sell everything, give it to the poor, and follow him, the man walks away defeated, "for he had many possessions" (Mark 10:22). Here we begin to see that *the Kingdom demands a new way of living.*

Finally, Mark makes clear that, as powerful as the Kingdom was in Jesus' ministry, it was only a beginning. He devotes a long section in chapter 13 to Jesus anticipating the future revelation of God's Kingdom upon earth beginning with the long-expected apocalyptic signs. Mark turns this mind-boggling scenario into a motivator for the disciples' wakeful watching (Mark 13:32–37): *the Kingdom will transform everything at an unexpected future time.*

Parables and Miracles

The parables and miracles of our Lord serve the purpose of conveying his teaching about the Kingdom. They do not merely prove Jesus' divinity or the truth of this message. They rather invite faithful and inquisitive hearers to understand and promote God's design for the age to come. In Jesus' miracles the powers of the future Kingdom of God are at work; but one must look past their external features in order to penetrate them as signs pointing to the Kingdom. To k amazed at Jesus' powers is not faith, for the Kingdom is about tough realities that require dedication and trust. One must entrust oneself to the one who is performing the deed, as several characters do in Mark. In this way the miracles become like visual parables that tell a story that one must enter into and make one's own. Faith may invite the miracle, but understanding completes it.

The parables are Jesus' most distinctive verbal teaching tool. All by themselves they make him a great figure in the history of education, quite apart from his status as a Messiah, Savior, and Lord. Parables make comparisons between daily life and the realities of the Kingdom. If we hear them properly, we enter into the dynamic of the comparison or story by completing the picture they begin to create. So we must become personally invested in them in order to understand them. Parables work like a kind of trap, surprising us toward insights that we might otherwise have resisted if their truth had been more directly stated. Read the classic Old Testament parable Nathan tells to David (2 Samuel 12) that shocks the king into confronting his own guilt.

Now, we might think that the parables were like illustrations to help make the Kingdom easier to comprehend. Actually, in Mark's Gospel account, Jesus used parables *not to make the Kingdom easier to understand, but harder!* What's the logic here? We might say the parables use a kind of reverse psychology whereby the confusing imagery darkens the Kingdom's mystery and excludes the casual listener. As a result it intensifies (for some anyway) the desire to understand and be included. The parables prompted outsiders to become insiders, which is the exact condition necessary for becoming part of the Kingdom. If so, the obscurity of the parables acted as a kind of screening device to ward off the uncommitted and merely half-interested window-shopper, and to reward the true seeker.

Mark Proclaims Jesus—He Saved Others; He Cannot Save Himself

The very first verse of Mark leaves no doubt about the focus he wants for his Gospel account: "The beginning of the gospel of Jesus Christ, [the Son of God]" (Mark 1:1). Right out of the gate we're given three names or titles that orient our reading to Jesus' identity: "Jesus," "Christ," and "Son of God."

"Jesus": As I've suggested, names were important in the ancient world. The English version of our Lord's name comes from the Latin *Iesus*, which is a translation of the Greek *Iesous*. They both ultimately derive from the Hebrew *Yehoshua*, a compound name later shortened to *Yeshua*, which means "The LORD saves." The root letters relate to the names Joshua and Hosea. Salvation is thus etched into the very lettering of our Lord's name.

"Christ": The English comes from the Latin *Christus*, a form of the Greek *Christos*, which in turn translates the Old Testament concept of *mashiah*, "the Anointed One," which English transliterates as "messiah." This title was first used for the "anointed ones," Israel's kings and priests, and was later transferred to the one expected to usher in the age to come. The ancient root of the idea lies in the royal son of David from Isaiah (Isaiah 9:1–6, 11:1–5). However, the title is much more complex in Mark, for he combines it with images of the Suffering Servant and the apocalyptic Son of Man.

"Son of God": This title also derives from the Old Testament, above all from the promise of an everlasting dynasty to King David. God promised to David that a child from his line should always occupy the throne of Israel, and that "I will be a father to him, and he shall be a son to me" (2 Samuel 7:14). "Son of God" was thus a royal title. Jesus clearly claims the title throughout his life on earth by cor tinually calling God his "Father." He does so in an intimate way, ca ing him "Abba" (Mark 14:36). Jesus' identity as Son of God g beyond royal titles and suggests something shocking to a Jewish sibility: a divine status. So closely does Jesus identify with Gc

for Mark, what Jesus does, God does. Moreover, that divine identity emerges most clearly, though unexpectedly, not in Jesus' works of power, but in his Death. For the climax of the Passion, as Jesus' head drops in death, then and only then does a human voice—and the voice of an outsider at that—speak the truth about his identity: "Truly this man was the Son of God!" (Mark 15:39).

We have to note three aspects about the revelation of Jesus' identity in Mark: its exact features were not expected, the hints about it were misunderstood, and the truth only partially dawned on the disciples. Mark puts a literary strategy to work here. He is undoubtedly drawing on the actual confusion around understanding Jesus when he was on earth. But Mark is also trying to coach his readers who have their own difficulties with Jesus' identity. Many scholars think Mark was writing to a community under persecution who thought of suffering as something contradictory to Christian faith in the resurrected Jesus. Mark reminds his readers that the Passion was neither an accident, nor an interruption, nor a contradiction to Jesus' divinity, in fact just the opposite. It captured the essence of the Gospel itself, because it was the deep revelation of Jesus' deepest identity rooted in humility and service. Moreover, at the same time it revealed the core of true discipleship.

Let's consider Mark's literary strategy. He casts the gradual unveiling of Jesus' identity like a mystery story that requires a kind of detective work. He builds tension into the narrative that keeps one involved and turning the page to find out what happens next. Mark arranges his story so that the reader knows about Jesus' identity from the beginning, but the other characters do not. You can see this for yourself if you work through the Gospel account with a question in mind: Who recognizes Jesus' identity and who doesn't? Take a piece of paper and draw a line down the middle for two columns. At top left column, write, "Knows Jesus," and at the top right column, "Doesn't Know Jesus." Now go through Mark's Gospel account listing the names of people or groups who fit in either column. The surprise is that the people we would most expect to know Jesus do not, whereas some incidental characters do recognize him. For Mark, Jesus' Death is a particularly dramatic moment of revelation; the Roman centurion standing at the Cross sees clearly who Jesus is.

Failure and Success as Disciples Great and Small

Mark's Gospel, like the other Gospel narratives, watches the disciples very closely, but their story does not follow the path we might expect. Instead of being heroic figures, they are flawed like the rest of us. This injects a realistic note into our fantasies that we might have been good followers if we had known Jesus face-to-face.

Actually, the flawed disciples are more like us. Mark presents scenes such as the original call of the disciples (Mark 1:16–20) and also the calling of the Twelve for their mission (3:13–15) that portray their obedience, courage, and faith; but other passages present a different and more disturbing picture. I've already alluded to a few: the disciples' inability to understand the Parable of the Sower (Mark 4:10: "The Twelve questioned him about the parables") or to identify Jesus' divinity as he stilled the storm (4:41: "Who is this . . . ?"). In another instance, they failed to understand what was happening when Jesus fed five thousand people in the wilderness (Mark 6:52: "they had not understood, . . . their hearts were hardened"). The situation came to a head after Jesus feeds another huge crowd of four thousand and has a strange conversation with the disciples as they cross the lake (Mark 8:14–21). Mark notes that the disciples had forgotten to bring bread with them into the boat, and they had only one loaf. When Jesus speaks metaphorically about the dangers of the "leaven" of the Pharisees and Herod, the disciples think he's talking about literal bread. Like a teacher frustrated with students who just flunked the midterm exam, Jesus comes closer to losing his cool than anywhere in the Gospel accounts: "Why do you conclude," he groans, "that it i because you have no bread? Do you not yet understand or compr hend? Are your hearts hardened?" (Mark 8:17). He recounts lessons (Mark 8:18–20). When he fed the five thousand, how many baskets did they pick up? Twelve, they said. When he fed the four thousand, how many baskets did they pick up? Seven, they said. He replied, "Do you still not understand?" (Mark 8:21).

Mark symbolically places this awkward scene just before Jesus heals a blind man, immediately after which he asks his searching identity question ("Who do you say that I am?"), followed by Peter's half understood response, "You are the Messiah" (8:22–29). Many scholars would see this sequence of scenes as the opening of a long section of Jesus privately teaching the disciples—a sequence that runs through the end of chapter 10. Mark's artistry makes this section serve double duty: it teaches readers about true discipleship, and also intensifies the irony and befuddlement that will lead to the disciples' later decline and final breakdown. They want glory and happiness without cost (Mark 10:35–41) and misplace their priorities ahead of the Passion (Mark 14:4–5). But to crown all, the disciples fail the ultimate test of their commitment when one betrays Jesus, another denies him, and they all desert him. However, hope glimmers faintly in the darkest hour when Jesus, even while predicting the disciples' disheartening fall, also declares, "After I have been raised up, I shall go before you to Galilee" (Mark 14:28). Furthermore, we must remember that Mark wrote his Gospel account in a time when Peter and all the other Apostles (Judas excepted) had proven their ultimate discipleship by the sacrifice of their lives.

To achieve his purpose of teaching discipleship, Mark skillfully introduces a series of so-called minor characters that illustrate the faithful aspects of discipleship that the main disciples do not: Take, for example, the way Mark teaches faith by cleverly intertwining two stories in chapter 5, the healings of Jairus' daughter and of the woman with the hemorrhage (Mark 5:21–43). We must see Mark not merely piling up miracle stories, but teaching about the faith of the people so open to Jesus' healings. Other characters follow who qualify as models of discipleship: a blind man throws off social niceties to receive sight (Mark 10:46–52); Simon the Cyrenian carries his Cross

(Mark 15:21); Joseph of Arimathea buries him (15:43–45). But many of the faithful are women, showing not only Jesus' favor toward women (a theme that both Luke and John pick up on), but also God's concern with those from whom men expected little of significance. A Gentile woman persists in seeking healing for her daughter (7:24–30); a widow offers little more than a mere few cents into the Temple treasury, yet she becomes a model for the disciples when "she, from her poverty, has contributed all she had, her whole livelihood" (Mark 12:44); and Mary Magdalene, Salome, Mary, the mother of Joses, and other women are witnesses at the Cross and the tomb (Mark 15:40–41; 16:1).

But the crowning figure among these minor characters is a woman who appears at the beginning of the Passion (Mark 14:3–9). When Jesus was at supper "a woman came with an alabaster jar of perfumed oil, costly genuine spikenard. She broke the alabaster jar and poured it on his head" (Mark 14: 3). Jesus solemnly declares, "She has anticipated anointing my body for burial. Amen, I say to you, wherever the gospel is proclaimed to the whole world, what she has done will be told in memory of her" (Mark 14:8–9). This unnamed disciple stands at the pinnacle of Mark's portrayal of true discipleship for readers of all ages to emulate.

CHAPTER 16

The Gospel According to Matthew: I Have Come Not to Abolish but to Fulfill

Read: Matthew 5–7; 16:13–20.

Matthew pays strong attention to Jewish views and values, evident in three themes (among others): the fulfillment of the old covenant in the new covenant, the dignity of the community of faith, and the ethical participation in the Kingdom.

Fulfillment of the Ancient Covenant

Many scholars see the Gospel according to Matthew (the name is traditional; we don't know who wrote it) emerging from a circle of converted Jewish scribes in Syria in the 80s of the first century. They knew the ancient Scriptures of Israel well and wanted to show how Christ "fulfilled" them—an important word in this Gospel. Five times during the story of Jesus' birth, Matthew refers to the Old Testament to show that events in his narrative "took place to fulfill what the Lord had said through the prophet" (1:22; see also 2:15, 17, 23). The work of fulfillment in Matthew does *not* abolish ancient laws or retire Old Testament prophecies or forget Israel's history. Rather, fulfillment reaffirms the earlier aspects even while setting them in e wider frame of Jesus' messianic mission, and lets the old cove- t come to fruition in the new. In the Lord's own words: "Do not think that I have come to abolish the law or the prophets. I have come not to abolish but to fulfill" (Matthew 5:17).

In this perspective, the Lord's own actions and words bring out the deepest intention of the Law and Prophets. We see this when a scribe asks Jesus to name the greatest commandment (Matthew 22:34–40). He answers that the greatest commandment speaks of loving God with all one's heart, soul, and mind (quoting Deuteronomy 6:5), while a second "like it" commands us to love one's neighbor as oneself (quoting Leviticus 19:18). Jesus clearly reaffirms the old covenant, and the old covenant's religious and ethical standards continue to obligate the followers of Jesus.

The Lord's own actions and words bring out the deepest intention of the Law and Prophets.

Moreover, all the old covenant's history, rituals, and doctrinal teachings anticipated the full revelation to come with Christ and they continue to instruct Christians. For example, after the Holy Family had escaped to Egypt to avoid the wrath of King Herod, an angel appeared to Joseph calling them back to Israel. Matthew comments that this "fulfilled" the Word of God spoken through the prophet Hosea, "Out of Egypt I called my son" (Hosea 11:1; Matthew 2:15). In its original context, these words plainly referred to the nation of Israel emerging as God's Chosen People ("my son") under Moses during the Exodus, while in Matthew they speak of Jesus. Matthew in no way dismisses the Exodus; rather he uncovers how events of ancient Israel continue powerfully to influence and inform the salvation story's climactic moment in the life of Jesus. That Jesus' life so poetically and spiritually "rhymes" with events in Israel's history points to the pattern of fulfillment in Matthew wherein Jesus replays and renews and sometimes reverses the history of Israel.

The Christian Community around Peter

Matthew specially emphasizes the Apostles as exalted heads of Jesus' future community, the Church—though without downplaying their failures shown by Mark. Versions of this theme appear in all four Gospel accounts, but Matthew alone uses the word "church" (*ekklesia*). He sees this community continuing and fulfilling "the assembly of the LORD" mentioned in the old covenant (for example, in Deuteronomy 23:3). He even pictures Jesus installing the Twelve Apostles as heads of the twelve renewed tribes of Israel in God's Kingdom (Matthew 19:28). This esteem for the new community extends particularly to Peter, who is a special focus of Matthew. Stories told about him in Matthew are found nowhere else, such as the episode of Peter walking on water, a story of his great faith mixed with great weakness (14:28–31). Most striking is Peter's confessional reply to Jesus' question, "Who do you say that I am?" (16:13–20). Peter responds, "You are the Messiah, the son of the living God" (16:16). Readers of Mark immediately notice two changes to Mark's story. In Matthew, Peter makes a full-throttle Christian confession of Jesus' divine identity. This is part of Matthew's interesting adjustment of Mark's dismal portrayal of thickheaded disciples. Why did he do this? For one thing, Matthew, a teacher, wants his readers to perceive Jesus as a *good* teacher—to see that Jesus is successful in getting his message across. But he also wants to ensure that we see the Apostles, future leaders of the Church, at least *partially* understanding Jesus' teaching.

Matthew's second change to Mark's story is less subtle and more important. He adds something that would have been wildly out of place in Mark's narrative: Jesus commissions Peter to be the "rock" upon which Jesus "will build my church" (16:18), and gives to him "the keys to the kingdom of heaven" (16:19). He also bestows upon Peter the power of binding and loosing, the ancient equivalent of executive decision-making authority (though the same kind of authority is delegated to the whole community in Matthew 18:18). The text, not surprisingly, has had a huge impact on the Church's life and self-understanding. In Mark the disciples and Peter understood in depth only a little about Jesus' identity until the Resurrection. But Matthew brings the post-Resurrection confession of Jesus and later communities' reverence for Peter right into the time of Jesus' ministry.

Ethics in the Kingdom

Matthew emphasizes that disciples' attitudes must be worked out in external deeds. Believing is good, but it's just the start. Faith must change real life habits so as to bend them toward justice and love. This comes through strongly in the Lord's teaching in the so-called Sermon on the Mount (chapters 5–7); not a one-time sermon, this is a collection and summary of Jesus' major teachings.

Jesus says, "I tell you, unless your righteousness surpasses that of the scribes and Pharisees, you will not enter into the kingdom of heaven" (Matthew 5:20). Jesus is criticizing the religious attitude that dwells on external achievement while congratulating itself on its righteousness ("Take care not to perform righteous deeds in order that people may see them" [6:1]). Jesus constantly drives down to the root sense and rationale of the Law's prescriptions. Even when seeming to overturn Scripture itself, he is really trying to lift up Scripture's deepest principles. Take the famous law of retaliation from the Exodus covenant, "eye for eye, tooth for tooth" (Exodus 21:24). Jesus quotes it and says it is misunderstood if taken as a license for revenge. "But I say to you, offer no resistance to one who is evil. When someone strikes you on [your] right cheek, turn the other one to him as well"—a sort of cheek-for-cheek understanding of the text (Matthew 5:39). He inverts the traditional understanding, and makes the second "eye" and "tooth" a token of forgiveness. Jesus sees more going on in the law of retaliation than a mere means to satisfaction. The law both laid down religious principles and fashioned tools for constructing a just society. As such it was instituted to proportionally *limit* revenge, not to *license* it. For Jesus, the Kingdom draws on de principles of peace that are the taproot of all just laws.

CHAPTER 17

The Infancy Stories in Matthew and Luke: Born King of the Jews

Read: Matthew 1–2; Luke 1–2.

More than any other part of the Christian Bible, except possibly the Passion, the infancy narratives (Matthew 1—2; Luke 1—2) have inspired works of art, poetry, and music that reveal true sources of theology and spirituality. These are simply must-read chapters for every Christian, giving delight and nourishment to mind and heart.

Although our memories tend to intertwine the characters and events from the two Gospel accounts, the stories in Matthew and Luke are quite distinct—something that escapes most casual readers. Each has a different "script," perspective, and tone. First, each Gospel focuses on a different parent, Joseph in Matthew, and Mary in Luke. In Matthew the revelations from angels—obviously God's messengers—come to Joseph in dreams at night, whereas the angel Gabriel is a human-like daytime visitor to Mary. Matthew emphasizes the fulfillment of prophecies and events in Scripture, as we've seen. Prophecy and fulfillment pervade Luke's story as well, but using big picture parallels more than quotes: see the Old Testament imagery in Zechariah's song of salvation history (Luke 1:67–79), or the likeness between Mary's *Magnificat* (Luke 1:46–55) and the song of Samuel's mother Hannah (1 Samuel 2:1–10), or Gabriel's allusions to the promise of David's dynasty (2 Samuel 7:13–14) in announcing the conception of Mary's divine child (Luke 1:32–33).

Intriguingly, Matthew, thought to be "the Jewish Gospel," emphasizes Gentiles in his birth story, while Luke, perhaps the only Gentile New Testament writer, stresses his story's Jewishness. Matthew gives a key role to Gentiles: Magi, respected scientists of their day, the best of pagan wisdom. Matthew used the Magi to critique those who knew the Jewish Scriptures, yet overlooked the birth of the King prophesied in them; he contrasted such people to these Gentiles, who with nothing but star maps still discerned the great event. In this, Matthew envisions a universal Church, Jews and Gentiles together, that the Risen Lord will commend at the end of the Gospel ("Go, therefore, and make disciples of all nations," 28:19).

Luke, by contrast, carefully paints character portraits of people who are deeply Jewish in their practices and sensibilities. Zechariah and Elizabeth, the parents of John the Baptist, remind us of Abraham and Sarah. Joseph and Mary fulfill all the obligations of pious Jews in the birth of their first child. During the child's presentation in the Temple, Anna and Simeon play distinctive roles emphasizing that period's intense expectation of the fulfillment of promises to Israel. The exquisite words of Simeon, probably composed by Luke, capture the evangelist's deeply Jewish devotional spirit:

> Now, Master, you may let your servant go
> in peace, according to your word,
> for my eyes have seen your salvation,
> which you prepared in the sight of all the peoples,
> a light for revelation to the Gentiles,
> and glory for your people Israel.

(Luke 2:29–32)

Most striking is the difference in tone and perspective between the two stories. Matthew features an undercurrent of tragedy that colors the otherwise marvelous event of the Lord's birth. If set to music, Matthew's story would be in a minor key. A thread of doubt and sadness pervades the story line, even if divine intervention prevents utter catastrophe. The confusion around Mary's pregnancy softened by Joseph's uprightness and God's direction. Even the genealogy of chapter 1 seems to prophesy trouble, recalling stories of women in dark circumstances. Herod's murder of the children trumps everything for cruelty, and the Holy Family's escape to Egypt as refugees (invoking God's care for the displaced of all ages and places) only underscores the tone of danger and grief.

Luke, however, invites us into an atmosphere of joy. The wonder and lightness of heart in the story is captured by the angel who announces "good news of great joy that will be for all the people" that "today in the city of David a Savior has been born for you who is Messiah and Lord" (2:10–11). The angel exclaims, "Nothing will be impossible for God" (1:37), Mary "proclaims the greatness of the Lord" (1:46–55), baby John leaps for joy in Elizabeth's womb (1:44), and Zechariah's tongue is loosed for

Most striking is the difference in tone and perspective between the two infancy stories.

praise (1:67–79). Luke's narrative seems at times like a Broadway musical: people burst into song at the drop of a hat. Luke carefully staged all this, of course, to portray the great event. Just as carefully, Luke sidesteps the dark undertow of the story Matthew emphasizes. He almost never alludes to suffering; Gabriel never mentions the Cross in his prophecies to Mary about her glorious Son. However, Luke does allow a shadow to pass quickly through the story at one point. When his parents bring Jesus to the Temple for dedication, old Simeon pronounces an ominous prophecy:

> Behold, this child is destined for the fall and rise of many in Israel, and to be a sign that will be contradicted (and you yourself a sword will pierce) so that the thoughts of many hearts may be revealed." (2:34–35)

Taking this equally with all the marvels revealed to her, Luke comments, Mary "kept all these things, reflecting on them in her heart" (2:19; also 51). These Christmas stories deserve all the wonder and artistry they have inspired through the centuries.

CHAPTER 18

The Gospel According to Luke and the Acts of the Apostles: Today Salvation Has Come

Read: Luke 5–6; 10; 15; 19.

The sweep and grandeur of salvation history emerges clearly in the evangelist Luke's two-volume work, the Gospel according to Luke and its sequel, the Acts of the Apostles. With twenty-four and twenty-eight chapters, respectively, the fifty-two chapters of these two books take up more than a quarter of the New Testament. Many scholars have discerned in these works a three-part vision of the history of salvation.

The Prophecy of Salvation (Luke 1—2)

The first part of Luke's salvation history appears in the first two chapters of his Gospel account, which we've treated earlier to an extent under the infancy stories. Luke emphasizes prophecy and fulfillment. After an important prologue that spells out his method of carefully investigating the stories (1:1–4), Luke portrays memorable figures full of wonder, daring, and anticipation as God is about to fulfill the covenant's ancient promises. As mentioned, several characters recall the Old Testament and the very best of ancient Jewish devotion to God. The poetic songs of Mary, Zechariah, and Simeon brim with Old Testament images and themes relating to God's covenant promise of salvation. They summarize the period of prophecy when Israel awaited God's fulfillment of ancient promise

The Accomplishment of Salvation (Luke 3—24)

The second part of salvation history appears in the remaining chapters of Luke's Gospel account, and forms the center of Luke's story. For Luke, every word and deed of Jesus fulfills the salvation promises made to the ancient covenant people. While Luke shares many stories and sayings with Matthew and Mark, including the expectation of Jesus' return and the age to come, careful readers nevertheless notice Luke's shift of emphasis. Jesus' teaching about God's Kingdom has an ambiguous aspect pictured as "near," which is to say that mysteriously it is both "already here" and at the same time also "not yet here." Both aspects appear in all four Gospels. But on balance, we can say the "not yet" aspect appears more prominently in Matthew and Mark (with the "already here" aspect slowly emerging), and the "already here" aspect appears more in Luke and John (with the "not yet" aspect still visible but slowly receding). For Luke, the Kingdom's "already" aspect emphasizes its presence, along with the actual change and real justice that are transforming conditions right here and right now. Jesus says in Luke, "The coming of the kingdom of God cannot be observed, and no one will announce 'Look, here it is,' or 'There it is.' For behold, the kingdom of God is among you" (Luke 17:20b–21).

The visible effects of the already-present Kingdom emerge in the story of the little tax collector, Zacchaeus (Luke 19:1–10). When Jesus passed by, he looked up into the tree and said, "Zacchaeus, come down quickly, for *today* I must stay at your house" (19:5; emphasis added). This word "today" has a special resonance for Luke, as we'll see in a minute. This personal connection stirred the man's heart; Luke says he received Jesus "with joy" (Luke 19:6). Now the transformative effect takes hold and Zacchaeus becomes a different person. He says to the Lord: "Behold, half of my possessions, Lord, I shall give to the poor, and if I have extorted anything from anyone I shall repay it four times over" (Luke 19:8). In these cases the anticipation of the coming Kingdom is so strong that it relieves us of our burdens and relaxes our death grip on material possessions and worldly values. Paradoxically, the coming of the Kingdom makes the Kingdom come. Jesus' forgiveness changes Zacchaeus, and he announces, "*Today* salvation has come to this house because this man too is a descendant of Abraham" (Luke 19:9; emphasis added). And this is the whole point of Jesus coming, as he announces in an oracle-like statement that might serve as a key verse for the entire Gospel: "For the Son of Man has come to seek and to save what was lost" (Luke 19:10).

It was not the first time that Luke had emphasized this transformative dimension of Christ's advent, a dimension he signals through his distinctive and repeated use of the word "today" throughout the Gospel account. At the very beginning, an angel announces to the shepherds the Good News of Jesus' birth: "*Today* in the city of David a Savior has been born for you who is Christ and Lord" (Luke 2:11; emphasis added). Later, Jesus proclaims a text in his home synagogue that prophesies the beginning of his ministry of liberation: "*Today* this Scripture passage is fulfilled in your hearing" (4:21; emphasis added). And finally at the scene of Jesus' Crucifixion, a penitent thief asks Jesus to remember him in his Kingdom. Jesus replies, "Amen, I say to you, *today* you will be with me in Paradise" (23:43; emphasis added). Luke wants believers to realize that, because of Jesus, they savor many gifts of heaven right this minute.

The Proclamation of Salvation (Acts of the Apostles 1—28)

The third part of salvation history commences in the Acts of the Apostles and extends, Luke implies, until today. Jesus himself gives a geographical outline of the spread of the Gospel in world history. "You will be my witnesses," Jesus tells the Apostles, "in Jerusalem, throughout Judea and Samaria, and to the ends of the earth" (Acts 1:8). Indeed we should notice Luke's concern to show the global scope of the Christian vision. Notice the long geographical arc of his two-volume work, which stretches from the beginning in Jerusalem, the Holy City (indeed in the Holy of Holies of the Temple, Luke 1:5), all the way to its end with Paul proclaiming Christ's message to Jews and Gentiles in the pagan capital city of Rome (Acts 28:16–31). The mission launch point is the day of Pentecost, when thousands of Jews from all over the world have gathered in Jerusalem and become witnesses of the birth of the Church. The Holy Spirit falls upon the Apostles, who speak in all the languages of the earth. Peter preaches a blockbuster sermon announcing that Christ has fulfilled the ancient prophecies and ascended to Lordship at God's right hand, and three thousand people are baptized (Acts 2:14–41). The sweep of Luke's vision could hardly be more majestic. Acts has far more to offer than can be touched on here. Luke crafted an account that offers genuine spiritual insight as well as fascinating history.

CHAPTER 19

The Book of Revelation: Write What You See

Read: Revelation 1–5; 21–22.

The Sense of an Ending

Most New Testament narratives have a problem with endings. The best one is probably Matthew's. The Risen Christ reconnects with his disciples, instructs them to make disciples, to baptize, and to teach all nations; then he promises, "Behold, I am with you always, until the end of the age" (Matthew 28:16–20). Fade to black. A new era opens, but Matthew brings his story to rest with a three-point landing. Luke seems at first to do something similar; Jesus rises into heaven and the disciples give praise in the Temple, so his narrative ends where it began (Luke 24:50–53). But Luke continues with another volume, the Acts of the Apostles, where he actually changes the Ascension story somewhat (Acts 1:1–12). Moreover, Acts itself has no ending per se; it pictures Paul under house arrest, freely preaching Christ in Rome, but then just stops (Acts 28:30–31). John's Gospel account seems to have the perfect ending in chapter 20 with Thomas' climactic exclamation to the Risen Jesus, "My Lord and my God!" (John 20:28), and the closing statement about the Gospel's purpose (20:31). But the author of this account can't resist adding another appearance story, so the curtain rises again briefly for Jesus' encore in chapter 21. The least resolved story is Mark's. Most scholars believe the Gospel ended at 16:8 in dissonance and irresolution. The women run away from the tomb, "seized with trembling and bewilderment

A mysterious young man has announced that Jesus has risen, and ordered them to tell the disciples. But then the unresolved final chord: "They said nothing to anyone, for they were afraid." Most agree that the ending in 16:9–20 was added much later, precisely because of dissatisfaction with the lack of resolution at 16:8. But analysts today also think that irresolution was a part of Mark's strategy, growing out of a well-considered theology of mystery and a literary artistry that prized allusion, irony, and misdirection. If true, Mark is making a much larger point about Christian faith itself: Jesus has come, but the story is far from over.

The Book of Revelation ends the New Testament but doesn't bring the biblical story of salvation to conclusion. Instead, this magnificent and unsettling book is a telescopic lens to *look through*, to see where the story of salvation is still moving.

We see some beautiful images that seem to suggest the story is ending: John sees "a new heaven and a new earth," with "the holy city, a new Jerusalem, coming down out of heaven from God" (Revelation 21:1–2). The vision is obviously spectacular, but it is also not real—at least not yet. Revelation imagines this future ending to the story while still quite mired in the muddles of history. The very point of having a vision of the end like this is that it comes in the middle in order to keep us going. Jesus' final words are

"Son of Man with Seven Candlesticks," *Bamberg Apocalypse*, painted around 1000.

hopeful; "Yes, I am coming soon." John responds for all readers: Amen! Come, Lord Jesus!" (22:20). But history in all its bloody, tragic messiness trudges on; its story still being told. The vision of Revelation honors our lack of resolution, but gives tools and frameworks for moving through it all, using a pedagogy of symbolism.

With all its garish imagery, it seems strange that anyone needs convincing that the Book of Revelation uses symbolism. Yet some people resolutely refuse to see that this book resists literalism with all its might, using signs and images that seek to bring coded reassurance in a time of desperate weakness and persecution—one that distinctly lacks a resolution. But tension and irresolution are the natural habitat of hope. For all its violent imagery, Revelation's central message is *not* about disaster and death, but about the supreme victory that Jesus Christ has achieved in his Death and will consummate on a cosmic stage when salvation's story comes to a close.

A Dazzling Christ Speaks

Revelation revels in the beauty and majesty of Christ, acclaiming and celebrating him in an astounding song of praise:

> Worthy is the Lamb that was slain
> to receive power and riches, wisdom and strength,
> honor and glory and blessing.

(Revelation 5:11–12)

Here, at the end of Sacred Scripture, we return to Jesus, the pulsating center of the Bible, Lord of the cosmos and of history. John's vision of the exalted Christ in chapter 1, reprised in chapter 22, can be seen as the final Resurrection appearance of our Lord, though it vastly differs from the previous Resurrection appearance stories. For one thing, Jesus' appearance here is more dazzling and demanding than the others, as he studies us with his "eyes . . . like a fiery flame" (1:14). The appearance to John is also different in that he actually does not narrate a story, but gives a description of his experience. Unlike other Resurrection stories, John (like the prophet Ezekiel, whom he imitates) describes what he sees and hears and feels *in order to bring us into the vision with him.* John feels an intimate relationship to his readers, including you and me. Uniquely in the Bible, he addresses himself directly to us *as his readers*: "I, John, your brother, who share with you the distress, the kingdom, and endurance we have in Jesus" (Revelation 1:9).

Significantly, despite its obvious visual qualities, this culminating vision comes to us through writing and reading. Jesus orders John not simply to tell the vision, but to *write it down*. The equation between Jesus' presence and command and the written text is clear. "Write on a scroll what you see and send it to the seven churches" (1:11). The scroll, or book written by John that conveys the words of Christ to the churches mirrors the book that we read in worship, for as we've quoted so often from the Second Vatican Council in these pages, Christ himself is present in his Word. As participants in the vision with John, and hearers of the Word in which Christ is present, now it is we who write our stories as witnesses to the Risen Christ.

GLOSSARY

Actualization: a process for reading biblical texts that, while respecting their meaning in the ancient context, also brings them to bear upon present needs and questions.

Covenant: a central biblical idea suggesting the structure of the relationship between God and Israel—a relationship based on promises, stipulations, and exchange of responsibilities with rights and privileges.

Chesed: Hebrew for "love" characterized by steadfastness and faithfulness; used of God's love for Israel and of human loyalty to God and people.

Historical-Critical Method: an approach to biblical scholarship that employs the human sciences to study the human aspects of biblical texts. It was endorsed by the 1993 document, *The Interpretation of the Bible in the Church.*

Paschal Mystery: refers to the Passion, Death, Resurrection, and Ascension of our Lord Jesus Christ as an event that conveys the salvation of humanity.

Pentateuch: Greek for "five scrolls"; refers to the first five books of the Bible, the Torah, the Law of Moses.

Septuagint: Greek translation of the Hebrew Bible; begun third century BC; became the Old Testament of Christians.

Tetragrammaton: Greek for "four letters"; God's sacred covenant name, YHWH; used seven thousand times in the Hebrew Bible.

Torah: Hebrew for "teaching"; refers to the Law of Moses, sometimes to the whole Jewish Bible.

CHRONOLOGY OF CHURCH DOCUMENTS RELATED TO THE BIBLE

1893   *On the Study of Holy Scripture (Providentissimus Deus)*
(Pope Leo XIII)

1943   *On the Most Opportune Way to Promote Biblical Studies (Divino Afflante Spiritu)* (Pope Pius XII)

1964   *Instruction on the Historical Truth of the Gospels*
(Pontifical Biblical Commission)

1965   *Constitution on Divine Revelation (Dei Verbum)*
(Second Vatican Council)

1992   *Catechism of the Catholic Church* (Section I, Articles 1–3)

1993   *The Interpretation of the Bible in the Church*
(Pontifical Biblical Commission)

2001   *The Jewish People and their Sacred Scriptures in the Christian Bible*
(Pontifical Biblical Commission)

2010   *The Word of the Lord (Verbum Domini)* (Pope Benedict XVI)

Many documents of the Church, including those referred to in this book, can be found on the Vatican website. For a good basic collection in print, see *The Bible Documents*, ed. David Lysik (Liturgy Training Publications, reprint 2007). More detailed is *The Scripture Documents*, ed. Dean P. Bechard (Liturgical Press, 2002).

Annual "State of the Bible" survey compiled by the American Bible Society and the Barna Foundation can be found at http://www.americanbible.org /features/state-of-the-bible.

FOR FURTHER READING
—A SELECTIVE LIST

Study Bibles

The Catholic Study Bible. 2nd ed. Edited by Donald Senior, CP, and John J. Collins. New York: Oxford University Press, 2011. A basic resource, highly recommended with 600+ pages of sound introductory material that make it a bargain. Contains the approved *New American Bible, revised edition.*

The New Jerusalem Bible: Study Edition. Edited by Henry Wansbrough. Garden City, NY: Doubleday, 1985. Excellent introductions and study helps (though footnotes are in tiny type).

The Jewish Annotated New Testament. Edited by Amy-Jill Levine and Marc Z. Brettler. New York: Oxford University Press, 2011. I have used this volume with great profit; it examines the deep Jewishness of the first Christian writings.

Other Useful Resources

Brown, Raymond E., SS. *Christ in the Gospels of the Liturgical Year.* Collegeville, MN: Liturgical Press, 2008. Excellent collection of six slim volumes in one, including *A Crucified Christ in Holy Week* (1986), which can be purchased separately.

Casey, Michael. *Sacred Reading: The Ancient Art of Lectio Divina.* Liguori, MO: Liguori/Triumph, 1996. A fine, short introduction to praying with the Bible.

Frigge, Marielle, OSB. *Beginning Biblical Studies.* Rev. ed. Winona, MN: Anselm Academic, 2013. Helpful, concise introductory textbook that elaborates on perspectives offered here.

Harrington, Wilfred, OP. *Reading Mark for the First Time.* Mahwah, NJ: Paulist Press, 2013. A solid short study for a serious first reading of Mark's Gospel.

Johnson, Luke Timothy. *The Real Jesus*. San Francisco: HarperOne, 1997. Sorts out the scholarship on Jesus as a historical of figure. Clears up a lot of misconceptions. Fascinating.

———. *Living Jesus: Learning the Heart of the Gospel*. San Francisco: HarperOne, 2000. A fine follow-up book to the previous one on the composite New Testament image of Jesus.

Levine, Amy-Jill. *The Misunderstood Jew*. San Francisco: HarperOne, 2007. A lively historical and literary study from a Jewish perspective.

Magrassi, Mariano. *Praying the Bible: An Introduction to Lectio Divina*. Collegeville, MN: Liturgical Press, 1998. Another fine little book on praying with the Bible.

O'Keefe, John, and R. R. Reno. *Sanctified Vision: An Introduction to Early Christian Interpretation of the Bible*. Baltimore, MD: Johns Hopkins University Press, 2005. A readable orientation to reading the Bible with the early Church Fathers.

Paprocki, Joe. *The Bible Blueprint*. Chicago: Loyola Press, 2009. A good basic orientation for beginners. Also in Spanish.

Riches, John K. *The Bible: A Very Short Introduction*. New York: Oxford University Press, 2000. Misleading title; actually a look at the development, cultural importance, and history of interpreting the Bible.

Senior, Donald. *Jesus: A Gospel Portrait*. Rev. ed. Mahwah, NJ: Paulist Press, 1992. A rich basic study of Jesus in the Gospels.